A YEAR of *Thanksgiving*

A YEAR of Thanksgiving

Kathi Owens

XULON PRESS

Xulon Press
2301 Lucien Way #415
Maitland, FL 32751
407.339.4217
www.xulonpress.com

© 2020 by Kathi Owens

All rights reserved solely by the author. The author guarantees all contents are original and do not infringe upon the legal rights of any other person or work. No part of this book may be reproduced in any form without the permission of the author. The views expressed in this book are not necessarily those of the publisher.

Unless otherwise indicated, Scripture quotations taken from the King James Version (KJV)–*public domain.*

Printed in the United States of America.

ISBN-13: 978-1-6312-9909-4
Ebook ISBN-13: 978-1-6312-9910-0

PREFACE

For several years, during the month of November, posts on social media challenged you to post a thank you each day of the month. It came to me that this is something I should do daily. The Lord showers me with abundant blessings every day of the year. As I did my daily Bible reading, I began to record a thank you each day from Scripture, and thus this book was created.
I have focused each day on a Scripture that highlights one of God's many blessings. Each page includes a section for you to journal, to record blessings God has bestowed upon you. A Bible reading guide that will take you through reading the Bible in one year is at the bottom of each page.

I pray that this book helps you focus on the bounty God has granted you and that you will receive a blessing every day as you thank the Lord for His good and perfect gifts. God has been so good!

I dedicate this book to God the Father, Son and Holy Spirit and to Brother William Smith, pastor of Bethany Baptist Church for over 40 years, who is now with Jesus.

> "O come, let us sing unto the LORD: let us make a joyful noise to the rock of our salvation. Let us come before his presence with thanksgiving, and make a joyful noise unto him with psalms. For the LORD is a great God and a great King above all gods."
>
> Psalm 95:1-3

All Scriptures quoted in this book are from the King James Version of the Holy Bible

JANUARY 1

Jeremiah 42:5 "Then they said to Jeremiah, The LORD be a true and faithful witness between us, if we do not even according to all things for the which the LORD thy God shall send thee to us."

The LORD be a true and faithful witness. Have you ever had someone lie to you or about you, someone who deceives you, someone who makes a promise but then does not do as stated? This undoubtedly causes hurt feelings, anger, and other negative emotions. God, always a true and faithful witness, cannot lie (Titus 1:2). What a blessing we have in the Lord, who will never lie to us, who will always keep His promises. Thank you, Lord, for being such a wonderful and faithful God!

_____
_____
_____
_____
_____
_____
_____

Daily Reading: Genesis 1-3

JANUARY 2

Hosea 2:23 "And I will sow her unto me in the earth; and I will have mercy upon her that had not obtained mercy; and I will say to them which were not my people, Thou art my people; and they shall say, Thou art my God."

Thou art my people. This is a profound and awesome thought, that we are the people of the Lord. Have you considered what that means, to be a people of the King of Kings, the Lord of Lords? What blessings we have in Him—not just on this earth, but into eternity. Thank you, Lord, for making me one of your people, for THOU ART MY GOD!!

_____
_____
_____
_____
_____
_____
_____

Daily Reading: Genesis 4-6

JANUARY 3

Psalm 126:3 "The Lord hath done great things for us; whereof we are glad."

The Lord hath done great things for us. Can you even fathom the things the Lord has done for you? This verse was written concerning the Israelites who were released from captivity, and the joy that followed. Remember the joy you experienced after being saved, what a burden was lifted, you were released from the captivity of sin. Thank you, Lord, for the freedom and blessings of salvation!

_____
_____
_____
_____
_____
_____
_____
_____

Daily Reading: Genesis 7-9

JANUARY 4

1 Peter 1:16 "Because it is written, be ye holy; for I am holy."

Be ye holy. Have you ever considered yourself holy? The word used here is the Greek word **hagios**, meaning pure, morally blameless, or consecrated. At the moment you were saved, God set you apart and consecrated you for His high and holy purpose. You are unable to purify yourself, because of your sinful nature, but He consecrated you when Jesus died for you on the cross. Thank you, Lord, for holiness. Help me live a pure and morally blameless life!

Daily Reading: Genesis 10-12

JANUARY 5

Psalm 127:2 "It is vain for you to rise up early, to sit up late, to eat the bread of sorrows: for so he giveth his beloved sleep."

He giveth his beloved sleep. Do you sometimes spend nights sleepless, worrying or sorrowing over some event in your life? The Lord wants you to lean upon Him. Place your worries and troubles in His hands. He is the great Problem Solver and the Great Comforter. Once you have given all over to Him, sweet sleep comes. Thank you, Lord, for that wonderful restful sleep!

_____
_____
_____
_____
_____
_____
_____
_____

Daily Reading: Genesis 13-15

JANUARY 6

Jeremiah 3:15 "And I will give you pastors according to mine heart, which shall feed you with knowledge and understanding."

And I will give you pastors. Who brought the Word of God to you, that ignited the fire within you to know more of His Word? Understand that those who did were led of the Lord TO YOU! You were the target, and when the Word pierced your heart and you came to the realization that you were in need of a Savior, only then did you humble yourself to ask God for forgiveness of your sin. Thank you, Lord, for those you brought through my life who showed me and taught me your Word!

_____

_____

_____

_____

_____

_____

_____

Daily Reading: Genesis 16-18

JANUARY 7

Exodus 15:1 "Then sang Moses and the children of Israel this song unto the LORD, and spake, saying, I will sing unto the LORD, for he hath triumphed gloriously: the horse and his rider hath he thrown into the sea."

For he hath triumphed gloriously. From the days of deliverance of the Israelites from Egypt, to present day, we can see God providing victory over the enemies of the people He loves. When God's people are humbled before Him and obey His Word, He fights on their behalf. When God is on your side, you have a definite advantage! Thank you, Lord, for your great power and might, and for fighting on the side of righteousness!

___
___
___
___
___
___
___
___

Daily Reading: Genesis 19-21

JANUARY 8

John 4:26 "Jesus saith unto her, I that speak unto thee am he."

I that speak unto thee am he. Does God speak to you? The Living Word, the Bible, is God's voice. You may find a new jewel in His Word that never touched your heart before when reading a Scripture you have read numerous times. Isn't God's Word amazing in the way that happens? His Word is alive and full of treasures waiting to be discovered. Thank you, Lord, for giving me the Scriptures, your revelation of YOU!

Daily Reading: Genesis 22-24

JANURRY 9

Psalm 34:19 "Many are the afflictions of the righteous: but the LORD delivereth him out of them all."

Many are the afflictions of the righteous. Do you thank the Lord for afflictions? Do you see the blessings in trials and troubles? Tribulations humble you; they make you more sympathetic to others and show you who your friends are. They magnify the Lord's love for you. During times of great trial, the Lord reveals His strength, delivers you, and gives you that sweet peace that follows. Thank you, Lord, for the afflictions of this life, and for your wonderful love and care!

_____

_____

_____

_____

_____

_____

_____

Daily Reading: Genesis 25-27

JANUARY 10

Deuteronomy 30:9a "And the LORD thy God will make thee plenteous in every work of thine hand, in the fruit of thy body, and in the fruit of thy cattle, and in the fruit of thy land, for good..."

The LORD thy God will make thee plenteous. Most of us have abundant possessions beyond the basic needs required to live. Compare those things that are necessary to what you have been given by the Lord and you will see how blessed you are. Thank you, Lord, for the plenteous blessings, for how you have favored the work of my hand!

Daily Reading: Genesis 28-30

JANUARY 11

Acts 22:21 "And he said unto me, Depart: for I will send thee far hence unto the Gentiles."

I will send thee far hence unto the Gentiles. Throughout all the Old Testament, the people of God were His chosen, the Hebrews. Few Gentiles in the Old Testament were saved. In this Scripture, God chose Paul to go to the Gentiles. Without God's Word, we would remain lost and blind in this sinful world, with no hope of salvation. Paul traveled far and wide to take God's Word to the lost Gentiles. Thank you, Lord, for extending your free salvation to the Gentiles, for I am a Gentile who has been saved through the preaching of your Word!

Daily Reading: Genesis 31-33

JANUARY 12

2 Timothy 3:15 "And that from a child thou hast known the holy scriptures, which are able to make thee wise unto salvation through faith which is in Christ Jesus."

From a child thou hast known the holy scriptures. Were you, like Timothy, brought up in church, with parents who talked about the Word of God, who taught you Scriptural truths? Many have not had that advantage, and following salvation, had to "unlearn" things taught them as children. Did you memorize Scriptures or learn simple Bible songs? Were you taught the simple Sunday School lessons? What a foundation to build upon through your Christian life! Thank you, Lord, for the Christian foundations, for the teachings received as children!

Daily Reading: Genesis 34-36

JANUARY 13

Luke 7:16 "And there came a fear on all: and they glorified God, saying, That a great prophet is risen up among us; and, That God hath visited his people."

God hath visited his people. In this Scripture, the people see Jesus as a great prophet, not yet knowing this was truly the promised Messiah, the Son of God. God in fact did visit His people, in the person of Jesus Christ. What a wonder that God in the flesh walked this earth, among the commoners. Thank you, Lord, for sending your Son, Jesus, to walk among men!

Daily Reading: Genesis 37-39

JANUARY 14

John 6:63 "It is the spirit that quickeneth; the flesh profiteth nothing: the words that I speak unto you, they are spirit, and they are life."

The words that I speak unto you… they are life. The Bible is not just another book, written for your reading pleasure, or for your personal knowledge. The Scriptures were provided and preserved to give life. Through the Word you learn that you are a sinner in need of a Savior and who that Savior is. Through the preaching of the Bible you are saved. Thank you, Lord, for the Scriptures, for the life in your Word!

Daily Reading: Genesis 40-42

JANUARY 15

Lamentations 3:22-23 "It is of the LORD'S mercies that we are not consumed, because his compassions fail not. They are new every morning: great is thy faithfulness."

Great is thy faithfulness. If you have had a time in your life that a person you loved was unfaithful, this Scripture may become your anchor and your stronghold. Friends and loved ones are human, with human failings, and will reject you, betray you, and deceive you. But God is ever faithful. His mercies and compassions will never fail you. Thank you, Lord, for your faithfulness and love that never ends!

_____

_____

_____

_____

_____

_____

Daily Reading: Genesis 43-45

JANUARY 16

2 Timothy 2:21 "If a man therefore purge himself from these, he shall be a vessel unto honour, sanctified, and meet for the master's use, and prepared unto every good work."

He shall be a vessel unto honour. By accepting the name of Christ and turning from iniquity, God will make you a vessel unto honor—one used by Him for His glory! There is no work on this earth as great and honorable as the work of spreading God's Word to the lost. Thank you, Lord, for making me a vessel of honor!

_____

_____

_____

_____

_____

_____

_____

Daily Reading: Genesis 46-48

JANUARY 17

Psalm 91:11 "For he shall give his angels charge over thee, to keep thee in all thy ways."

He shall give his angels charge over thee. If you have ever had a close brush with danger, you may have felt God's protecting hand preventing certain injury or death. You probably are not aware of how many times you came close to disaster, missing by seconds a vehicle wreck, a personal attack, etc. God's angels watch over you, protecting and guiding you in your daily activities. Thank you, Lord, for your wonderful watch care!

Daily Reading: Genesis 49-50, Exodus 1

JANUARY 18

John 1:12 "But as many as received him, to them gave he power to become the sons of God, even to them that believe on his name."

To them gave he power to become the sons of God. Whether you were born to royalty, or a commoner, you became a son (or daughter) of God when you accepted Jesus as your Savior. Worldly possessions of this life are temporary and will be destroyed at the end of this life. The abundance provided to the children of God is eternal and will be more than our miniscule minds can fathom. Thank you, Lord, for choosing me as your own, for making me one of your children!

Daily Reading: Exodus 2-4

JANUARY 19

2 Timothy 2:10 "Therefore I endure all things for the elect's sakes, that they may also obtain the salvation which is in Christ Jesus with eternal glory."

I endure all things for the elect's sakes. To provide salvation Jesus suffered physically a horrendous death on the cross. He suffered greater agony when the Father turned His back on His Son. Separation from your earthly father brings hurt and pain, but separation from God the Father leads to a much greater anxiety and distress. Thank you, Lord, for enduring the pain on the cross that I might be saved eternally!

_____
_____
_____
_____
_____
_____
_____
_____

Daily Reading: Exodus 5-7

JANUARY 20

Philemon 1:4-5 "I thank my God, making mention of thee always in my prayers, hearing of thy love and faith, which thou hast toward the Lord Jesus, and toward all saints."

Hearing of thy love and faith. It brings joy to know that people you love are demonstrating their Christianity through their actions and activities. I recently connected with a cousin of mine who I had only met once in my life. Shortly after I connected with him on social media, he received a diagnosis from his doctor that he had just a few weeks to live. The outpouring of love to this man was amazing, so many of his friends commented of how he had touched their lives and was such a testimony to the love of Jesus. Thank you, Lord, for those who live for You, for those whose lives are pictures of your love and grace!

Daily Reading: Exodus 8-10

JANUARY 21

Hebrews 6:19 "Which hope we have as an anchor of the soul, both sure and steadfast, and which entereth into that within the veil."

We have as an anchor of the soul. Remember the days, before your salvation, when you seemed to drift to and fro, blown here and there by every wind. Aren't you glad to have that anchor today, that keeps you steady no matter what is happening in your life, in your community, in your world? Thank you, Lord, for that anchor, that secures no matter what comes my way!

Daily Reading: Exodus 11-13

JANUARY 22

Revelation 12:10 "And I heard a loud voice saying in heaven, Now is come salvation, and strength, and the kingdom of our God, and the power of his Christ: for the accuser of our brethren is cast down, which accused them before our God day and night."

Now is come salvation, and strength. When you are being accused falsely, you often feel weak and helpless, without control. Jesus is our salvation and our strength in these times, in our weakness He is made strong. We have no need to defend ourselves against the offenders, for He will judge them. Thank you, Lord, for your strength and power, for casting down the accusers!

_____
_____
_____
_____
_____
_____
_____

Daily Reading: Exodus 14-16

JANUARY 23

1 Thessalonians 1:9 "For they themselves shew of us what manner of entering in we had unto you, and how ye turned to God from idols to serve the living and true God."

How ye turned to God from idols to serve the living and true God. Before you were saved, were you an idol worshipper? I was. As a Christian converted from Catholicism, I see now that praying before the statues of Mary, St Francis of Assisi, St Christopher, etc., was idol worship. The Scriptures say there is one Mediator between God and man, and that is Jesus Christ. No place in the Bible does it indicate that saints in heaven take our petitions before God, only Jesus can do that. Thank you, Lord, for showing me many truths of Your Word, and for bringing me from idolatry to worship and praise only You!

_____

_____

_____

_____

_____

_____

Daily Reading: Exodus 17-19

JANUARY 24

1 John 2:20 "But ye have an unction from the Holy One, and ye know all things."

Ye have an unction from the Holy One. At the moment you were saved, you received the Holy Spirit from God, providing you power that is not possessed by the unsaved. This power gives you an understanding of Scripture, the strength to turn away from sin, and a connection with the Lord, like plugging into an electrical outlet. Thank you, Lord, for this anointing, and for your power!

Daily Reading: Exodus 20-22

JANUARY 25

1 Timothy 6:8-9 "And having food and raiment let us be therewith content. But they that will be rich fall into temptation and a snare, and into many foolish and hurtful lusts, which drown men in destruction and perdition."

Having food and raiment let us be therewith content. The Lord provides us with the basic necessities of life, along with many abundant blessings, especially in these United States. With spiritual maturity comes contentment, and the loss of longing for the material things of this world. Riches often cause worry and become snares or traps. Thank you, Lord, for your provision, help me to be satisfied and content in you!

_____
_____
_____
_____
_____
_____
_____
_____

Daily Reading: Exodus 23-25

JANUARY 26

John 14:2-3 "In my Father's house are many mansions: if it were not so, I would have told you. I go to prepare a place for you. And if I go to prepare a place for you, I will come again, and receive you unto myself; that where I am, there ye may be also."

I go to prepare a place for you. Oh, the wonders of Heaven, human minds cannot conceive the beauty and marvels of that place! And it is being prepared for you, a child of God. The physical beauty of Heaven is beyond human imagination, but the true wonder of Heaven is being in the presence of Jesus our Savior. Thank you, Lord, for the promise and hope of this eternal home, Heaven!

Daily Reading: Exodus 26-28

JANUARY 27

Exodus 7:5 "And the Egyptians shall know that I am the LORD, when I stretch forth mine hand upon Egypt, and bring out the children of Israel from among them."

And the Egyptians shall know that I am the LORD. Just as God judged Egypt, judgment is coming to those who have rejected Christ, when they will see the great wrath of God. There will be no unbelievers at that time, as all will know that God is real, but for those lost, it will be too late—they will know that "I am the LORD". Thank you, Lord, for the saving knowledge of your Word, help me to be a faithful witness to those who are unsaved.

_____
_____
_____
_____
_____
_____
_____

Daily Reading: Exodus 29-31

JANUARY 28

1 Peter 5:7 "Casting all your care upon him; for he careth for you."

He careth for you. What a wonder that God cares for you. He who made the earth, the stars, the planets, the suns, the solar systems, all the animals and living creatures—He cares for YOU! He is the God of all creation, the One who has always been, with no beginning and no end—He cares for YOU! Thank you, Lord, for your love and protection, for considering me an important part of your creation!

Daily Reading: Exodus 32-34

JANUARY 29

Micah 7:18 "Who is a God like unto thee, that pardoneth iniquity, and passeth by the transgression of the remnant of his heritage? he retaineth not his anger for ever, because he delighteth in mercy."

He delighteth in mercy. Mercy is an act of compassion, not meting punishment where punishment is due. If God were not a God of mercy you would be heading right into the pits of hell. God is pleased to extend mercy to those who call on Him in repentance and faith. Thank you, Lord, for your great mercy, my salvation!

Daily Reading: Exodus 35-37

JANUARY 30

Isaiah 64:8 "But now, O LORD, thou art our father; we are the clay, and thou our potter; and we all are the work of thy hand."

We all are the work of thy hand. You hear people say, "He is a self-made man". A self-made man or woman perhaps is considered successful in the eyes of this world. A believer is shaped by God, into a being that is like Him. We are unable to make ourselves like Him, but we can become like God when we conform to His will. Thank you, Lord, for being my potter, for shaping me and making me more and more like You!

Daily Reading: Exodus 38-40

JANUARY 31

2 Timothy 1:7 "For God hath not given us the spirit of fear; but of power, and of love, and of a sound mind."

God hath not given us the spirit of fear. Some people live in fear—alarmed by change and dreading the unknown. God has released us from fear, giving us power, love, and a sound mind! We have nothing to dread, as God is with us through every situation and moment of our lives. Thank you, Lord, for taking away fear, for giving me assurance that in all things, you are in control!

_____

_____

_____

_____

_____

_____

_____

Daily Reading: Leviticus 1-3

February 1

Amos 5:4 "For thus saith the Lord unto the house of Israel, Seek ye me, and ye shall live."

Seek ye me, and ye shall live. The plan of salvation is simple, so simple in fact, that many cannot accept that all required for salvation is to trust and believe in Jesus. Christ did it ALL on the cross, paying the price for your sins. Thank you, Lord, for the free gift of salvation. Thank you, Lord, that salvation is not dependent on me, for I am a lowly sinner, one who could never be acceptable to you without Christ!

_____
_____
_____
_____
_____
_____
_____

Daily Reading: Leviticus 4-6

February 2

Matthew 7:7 "Ask, and it shall be given you; seek, and ye shall find; knock, and it shall be opened unto you."

Ask, and it shall be given you. Take your petitions to the Lord, ask Him for the desires of your heart. Prove Him. Ask in HIS WILL, and he will give it to you. In the early days of my salvation, I had many questions about the Scripture, but I had no knowledge of study and reference Bibles. When I prayed that God would give me understanding of a particular Scripture, without exception and within days, our pastor or another preacher would touch on the subject in a message, giving me insight into what God had written. Thank you, Lord, for answered prayer. You are forever faithful!

Daily Reading: Leviticus 7-9

February 3

2 Peter 3:13 "Nevertheless we, according to his promise, look for new heavens and a new earth, wherein dwelleth righteousness."

Look for new heavens and a new earth. God tells in His Word that after Satan and his angels are banished to the pits of hell, He will create a new Heaven and a new earth, without sin, without death, a perfect place for His saints and angels. Sin, pain, separation, and death are so much a part of our lives on this earth that it is beyond our human imagination to think of a world without those things. Thank you, Lord, for this promise, of a place where I will dwell forever with You, a perfect place of peace and rest!

Daily Reading: Leviticus 10-12

February 4

Ephesians 3:17-19 "That Christ may dwell in your hearts by faith; that ye, being rooted and grounded in love, may be able to comprehend with all saints what is the breadth, and length, and depth, and height; and to know the love of Christ, which passeth knowledge, that ye might be filled with all the fullness of God."

And to know the love of Christ. Do you know the love of Christ? Over the days and years following salvation, you behold more and more of the love of Christ, and yet, this Scripture tells us that it passes our knowledge! No matter what we have experienced on this earth, we still have not seen all the love of Christ! Thank you, Lord, for Christ's wonderful love!

_____
_____
_____
_____
_____
_____

Daily Reading: Leviticus 13-15

February 5

Ephesians 4:13 "Till we all come in the unity of the faith, and of the knowledge of the Son of God, unto a perfect man, unto the measure of the stature of the fullness of Christ."

Till we all come in the unity of the faith. Life after salvation is a continuous sanctification process, always drawing closer to becoming that "perfect" man or woman (the word perfect in scripture means mature). At the time that you come in unity of the faith, you have reached the point that you accept God's Word as it is written, not trying to make it say what suits your life, and you do your best to live according to His Word. Thank you, Lord, for that sanctification process, drawing me ever nearer to the One who died for me!

Daily Reading: Leviticus 16-18

February 6

Psalm 55:22 "Cast thy burden upon the LORD, and he shall sustain thee: he shall never suffer the righteous to be moved."

Cast thy burden upon the LORD, and he shall sustain thee. Throughout life trials are so troublesome that they can nearly destroy a person. As a Christian you have someone who can hold you up, carry you through these times—Jesus! He wants you to cast your burden on Him, depend on Him, lean on Him, and take all your cares to Him. Oh, what a wonderful, loving Savior! Thank you, Lord, for your strength and care!

_____

_____

_____

_____

_____

_____

_____

_____

Daily Reading: Leviticus 19-21

February 7

Isaiah 52:7 "How beautiful upon the mountains are the feet of him that bringeth good tidings, that publisheth peace; that bringeth good tidings of good, that publisheth salvation; that saith unto Zion, Thy God reigneth!"

How beautiful... are the feet of him that bringeth good tidings. Do you remember the person who brought to you the Word of God, the Word that touched the deepest part of your heart, and brought you to a saving knowledge of Jesus Christ? One who stands out in my memory was a young teenage girl who wrote me a five-page letter, full of Scripture, that created in me a hunger to know the truth of God's Word. As a fourteen-year old girl, I began to read the Bible, searching for truth. Thank you, Lord, for those who share your Word, who take it to those nearby and to those in far-away lands!

_____
_____
_____
_____
_____
_____

Daily Reading: Leviticus 22-24

February 8

Matthew 13:16 "But blessed are your eyes, for they see: and your ears, for they hear."

Blessed are your eyes, for they see. The eyes of the saved have been opened by the Holy Spirit, giving the ability to read God's Word with understanding, and the capability to hear God's Word and apply it to the heart. As the man healed of blindness by Jesus said, "I was blind, now I see" (John 9:25). God's Word works in you as the Holy Spirit gives you the ability to see and to hear. Thank you, Lord, for working in me, taking away my blindness, and allowing me to see the blessed truths in your Word!

_____

_____

_____

_____

_____

_____

_____

Daily Reading: Leviticus 25-27

February 9

2 Thessalonians 1:6 "Seeing it is a righteous thing with God to recompense tribulation to them that trouble you."

Recompense tribulation to them that trouble you. Are you troubled by others because you are trying to live according to the will of God? This Scripture tells us that God will avenge the trouble brought upon you. You need not to become angry, stressed, or seek revenge with these tormenters. God will take care of them! Go on with life, put it all into God's hands. Thank you, Lord, for giving me peace in my heart as I live in this wicked world, knowing you have it under control!

_____
_____
_____
_____
_____
_____
_____

Daily Reading: Numbers 1-3

February 10

Genesis 1:3 "And God said, Let there be light: and there was light."

Let there be light. I have taught Sunday School for many years, and the account of God's creation is one of my favorite things to teach all ages of youth. God created the light on the first day and divided the light from the darkness. It is amazing that the light was created BEFORE the sun. Where did that light originate? It came from Jesus Christ—He is the light. Thank you, Lord, for sending your Son, Jesus, to bring light to this dark and dying world!

_____

_____

_____

_____

_____

_____

_____

Daily Reading: Numbers 4-6

February 11

John 14:26 "But the Comforter, which is the Holy Ghost, whom the Father will send in my name, he shall teach you all things, and bring all things to your remembrance, whatsoever I have said unto you."

Bring all things to your remembrance. Before you were saved you may have heard the Gospel of God's Word many times. Perhaps as a child you were taken to church and Sunday School and were taught Bible lessons and Scripture verses. Since you accepted Jesus as your Lord and Savior, those Scriptures you heard are often brought back to your mind with an understanding you did not have when they were first presented to you. With the Holy Spirit you have the ability to apply God's Word to your life. Thank you, Lord, for bringing your Word to life for me!

_____

_____

_____

_____

_____

Daily Reading: Numbers 7-9

February 12

Nehemiah 9:17 "And refused to obey, neither were mindful of thy wonders that thou didst among them; but hardened their necks, and in their rebellion appointed a captain to return to their bondage: but thou art a God ready to pardon, gracious and merciful, slow to anger, and of great kindness, and forsookest them not."

But thou art a God ready to pardon, gracious and merciful, slow to anger, and of great kindness. This Scripture speaks of God's mercy toward the Hebrew children. They turned against Moses and God, wishing to return to Egypt. They murmured against Moses, the leader God provided them. They made and worshipped an idol. They complained and showed no gratitude toward God for all He had done for them. And yet God displayed mercy, love, and kindness to the Israelites. He does the same for you and for me when we fail Him. Thank you, Lord, for being slow to anger, for your pardon and forgiveness of all my sins, which are many!

Daily Reading: Numbers 10-12

February 13

2 Chronicles 32:8 "With him is an arm of flesh; but with us is the LORD our God to help us, and to fight our battles. And the people rested themselves upon the words of Hezekiah king of Judah."

With us is the LORD our God to help us, and to fight our battles. Perhaps you are fighting battles today. Whether they are physical, mental, spiritual, financial, you are not abandoned. Often you may feel you are alone in your battles because no one understands what you are experiencing. Just remember God is there on your side. "If God be for us, who can be against us?" (Romans 8:31) Thank you, Lord, for fighting my battles. With You I am strong and brave!

_____
_____
_____
_____
_____
_____
_____

Daily Reading: Numbers 13-15

February 14

John 15:9 "As the Father hath loved me, so have I loved you: continue ye in my love."

As the Father hath loved me, so have I loved you. An earthly father has a special love for his children, but it is an imperfect love. God the Father has a special love for Christ, a perfect love unlike any other. And here, Jesus states that He has loved us like God the Father loves Him. Thank you, Lord, for your love, a perfect love, so deep that You were willing to suffer death on the cross that I may be saved!

Daily Reading: Numbers 16-18

February 15

Revelation 2:10 "Fear none of those things which thou shalt suffer: behold, the devil shall cast some of you into prison, that ye may be tried; and ye shall have tribulation ten days: be thou faithful unto death, and I will give thee a crown of life."

Be thou faithful unto death, and I will give thee a crown of life. In this life you have many trials and troubles. But you have this blessed promise: that if you are faithful to Christ, you will receive a crown of life, and glory forever with the One who died for you! You choose your reaction to trials. Use trials to draw closer to Jesus, seek His strength when you are weak. Know that there are greater blessings for you in days to come. Thank you, Lord, for the trials and suffering, for great reward is in my future!

_____

_____

_____

_____

_____

_____

Daily Reading: Numbers 19-21

February 16

Psalm 63:7 "Because thou hast been my help, therefore in the shadow of thy wings will I rejoice."

In the shadow of thy wings will I rejoice. Christians become more and more a minority in the world, and persecution and prosecution of Christians are widely accepted practices. Have you been singled out by co-workers or neighbors because of your faith? Do you have non-Christian friends, neighbors or acquaintances who at times make you a target for unfair or hostile treatment? Comfort yourself in the shadow of our Lord's wings. He is our true Friend and Defender. Thank you, Lord, for being my help during times that I feel alone and troubled and for protecting me in the shadow of your wings!

_____
_____
_____
_____
_____
_____

Daily Reading: Numbers 22-24

February 17

2 Timothy 4:17 "Notwithstanding the Lord stood with me, and strengthened me; that by me the preaching might be fully known, and that all the Gentiles might hear: and I was delivered out of the mouth of the lion."

The Lord stood with me and strengthened me. With Christ, there is nothing you cannot do, nothing is impossible. Seek help from Jesus when you are overwhelmed with work and responsibilities. He will take you through it. He will take away the stress and give you the time and the strength to endure. Thank you, Lord, for helping me when it seems I cannot possibly make it through the day, when the work that needs completed is greater than human ability. You give me the energy, the knowledge and the endurance!

_____

_____

_____

_____

_____

_____

Daily Reading: Numbers 25-27

February 18

Psalm 147:4 "He telleth the number of the stars; he calleth them all by their names."

He calleth them all by their names. Take the time to really look at the night sky when it is clear and full of stars. The number of stars is huge, and that number is just what you can see with your naked eye or a telescope. There are many more that may be seen using more advanced technology. And God tells the number and calls them all by name. What a great God we serve! Thank you, Lord, for your greatness; I wonder at your omniscience and your power!

_____

_____

_____

_____

_____

_____

_____

Daily Reading: Numbers 28-30

February 19

Isaiah 25:8 "He will swallow up death in victory; and the Lord GOD will wipe away tears from off all faces; and the rebuke of his people shall he take away from off all the earth: for the LORD hath spoken it."

He will swallow up death in victory. Many fear the thought of dying, of reaching that day when they draw their last breath. As a believer in Jesus, there is no need for fear. Physical death will give way to eternal life, a perfect and glorious life in the presence of Jesus Christ, sharing His glory. Death will be a victory—no more pain, no sorrow, no sin. Thank you, Lord, that I can look forward to that time that I pass from this life into Your magnificent presence!

_____
_____
_____
_____
_____
_____

Daily Reading: Numbers 31-33

February 20

Isaiah 25:8 "He will swallow up death in victory; and the Lord GOD will wipe away tears from off all faces; and the rebuke of his people shall he take away from off all the earth; for the LORD hath spoken it."

The Lord GOD will wipe away tears from off all faces. I cry so easily, sometimes I even cry over commercials! The day is coming when there will be no more tears. What a wonderful time that will be! Then we will accept God's perfect will in all that has occurred on this earth, and all will be well. Thank you, Lord, for that blessed hope of a perfect and wonderful eternity!

Daily Reading: Numbers 34-36

February 21

I Corinthians 6:20 "For ye are bought with a price: therefore glorify God in your body, and in your spirit, which are God's."

For ye are bought with a price. How much would it cost to buy you salvation? There is only one acceptable price for the forgiveness of sins, the death of the perfect sacrifice, Jesus Christ. Thank you, Lord Jesus, for willingly going to the cross, for paying the price for my sins!

Daily Reading: Deuteronomy 1-3

February 22

Psalm 94:19 "In the multitude of my thoughts within me thy comforts delight my soul."

Thy comforts delight my soul. Are you burdened with worries and troublesome thoughts? Does the news of war, sickness, sin, and corruption lay heavy upon your heart? Do things happening within your family or church make you anxious? Drawing near to the Lord in prayer and the reading of His Word will bring comfort and peace to your soul. Thank you, Lord, that amid trials and troubles I can rest assured that you are still in control!

_____
_____
_____
_____
_____
_____
_____
_____

Daily Reading: Deuteronomy 4-6

February 23

Philippians 4:11 "Not that I speak in respect of want: for I have learned, in whatsoever state I am, therewith to be content."

I have learned...to be content. The closer a person comes to the Lord, the less important are the things of this earth. Contentment is found and satisfaction wipes out the longing for material things. As a young person, I had difficulty understanding why a young couple would go to a third world country as missionaries, leaving behind what I thought was a great life here in the U.S. I now know that those people had reached a spiritual maturity far beyond mine. Thank you, Lord, for the contentment I now have in you, not seeking things, but seeking to know you on a higher level!

_____
_____
_____
_____
_____
_____

Daily Reading: Deuteronomy 7-9

February 24

2 Corinthians 4:6 "For God, who commanded the light to shine out of darkness, hath shined in our hearts, to give the light of the knowledge of the glory of God in the face of Jesus Christ."

God… hath shined in our hearts, to give the light of the knowledge of the glory of God. Do you recall the dark days before you were saved? Did you struggle with finding a purpose and path for your life? Were there days that life seemed hopeless? Most of us have experienced that feeling. But when the light of the Gospel shined in, and you came to know Jesus, you discovered a marvelous expectation that a better day is coming. Thank you, Lord, for that knowledge, that hope, that promise of a wonderful, eternal life in your presence!

_____
_____
_____
_____
_____
_____
_____

Daily Reading: Deuteronomy 10-12

February 25

Psalm 73:26 "My flesh and my heart faileth: but God is the strength of my heart, and my portion for ever."

God is the strength of my heart. The heart is the life of the body. When the heart fails, the body cannot function. If the heart's strength is not restored, the body dies. God is the strength of our spiritual heart, and when we sin and turn from God, we become weak in the spirit, making it difficult to even pray. When we are in a right relationship with God, seeking Him in all that we do, He gives us strength to overcome sin and to live according to His will and His Word. Thank you, Lord, for the spiritual strength you provide!

_____

_____

_____

_____

_____

_____

_____

Daily Reading: Deuteronomy 13-15

February 26

Titus 2:11 "For the grace of God that bringeth salvation hath appeared to all men."

Salvation hath appeared to all men. The knowledge of God has been brought before all men in God's creation. The earth reveals the glory and greatness of God, in the mountains and canyons, in the sun, moon and stars, in the life that springs forth across all the earth. Nature is a revelation of the Creator. Thank you, Lord, for the beautiful world you have given me. Thank you for the revelation of yourself in the world. Thank you for my salvation, the free gift of mercy and grace!

Daily Reading: Deuteronomy 16-18

February 27

Genesis 1:26 "And God said, Let us make man in our image, after our likeness: and let them have dominion over the fish of the sea, and over the fowl of the air, and over the cattle, and over all the earth, and over every creeping thing that creepeth upon the earth."

And God said, Let us make man in our image, after our likeness. We were created in God's image; we are like God! As God is Father, Son and Holy Spirit, we are body, soul, and spirit. Man was created without sin, but then fell into sin. God gave man dominion over the animals, over every creature on the earth, as He has dominion over man. Thank you, Lord, for creating me in your likeness, and thank you that I can become more like you as I seek and follow your will!

Daily Reading: Deuteronomy 19-21

February 28

1 Corinthians 1:27 "But God hath chosen the foolish things of the world to confound the wise; and God hath chosen the weak things of the world to confound the things which are mighty;"

God hath chosen the foolish things of the world to confound the wise. Man has developed all sorts of theories about the origin of the earth and of man, using man's intelligence to show that creation by God is untrue, a fable, a foolish belief. But every theory developed by man is proven untrue through God's Word and the wonders of nature. Thank you, Lord, for your Word and your creation, that proves your existence and your goodness!

Daily Reading: Deuteronomy 22-24

February 29

2 Corinthians 9:15 "Thanks be unto God for his unspeakable gift."

Thanks be unto God for his unspeakable gift. The word unspeakable is the same as indescribable, or unable to relate in words. And this says *gift,* not gifts. What is our unspeakable gift? It is the free salvation that provides joy and peace and love, eternal life with the Lord, and so much more. Thank you, Lord, for this unspeakable gift!

Daily Reading: Deuteronomy 25-27

March 1

1 Timothy 6:6 "But godliness with contentment is great gain."

Godliness with contentment. After salvation, a Christian should grow closer to the Lord each day through prayer, Bible reading, and in serving Him in daily life—the process of sanctification. There comes a time when you realize that all the happiness and joy you have sought in life are yours through the Lord, and the longing for other things is nearly diminished. Thank you, Lord, that I can reach a point of contentment, when like a cat, I am satisfied and curled up in your arms, with all the desires of my heart fulfilled in You!

Daily Reading: Deuteronomy 28-30

March 2

Psalm 34:15 "The eyes of the LORD are upon the righteous, and his ears are open unto their cry."

His ears are open unto their cry. The God who created the universe, the all-powerful, all knowing God has His ears open to your cry. Your exclamation of sorrow, pain, confusion, repentance, or need is heard by God. Thank you, Lord, for hearing my every plea. You have heard my cry and provided comfort, relief, understanding, and forgiveness, and have met my every need!

_____

_____

_____

_____

_____

_____

_____

Daily Reading: Deuteronomy 31-34

March 3

Deuteronomy 28:7 "The LORD shall cause thine enemies that rise up against thee to be smitten before thy face: they shall come out against thee one way, and flee before thee seven ways."

The LORD shall cause thine enemies that rise up against thee to be smitten. We all have enemies. They may be people but may also be temptations that cause you to fall into sin. Satan knows your weaknesses, and attacks where he knows you are most vulnerable. Thank you, Lord, that with you on my side, I can overcome any foe, and the enemy will flee seven ways!

Daily Reading: Joshua 1-3

March 4

Deuteronomy 32:4 "He is the Rock, his work is perfect: for all his ways are judgment: a God of truth and without iniquity, just and right is he."

He is the Rock, his work is perfect. We have a perfect God, One who not only gives life, but who loved us enough to provide a Savior. His judgments are perfect. Every sin must be paid for. We are imperfect sinners who could never make it to Heaven in our own efforts. Thank you, Lord, for being my Rock and my salvation, and for your mercy and love!

Daily Reading: Joshua 4-6

March 5

1 Thessalonians 2:13 "For this cause also thank we God without ceasing, because, when ye received the word of God which ye heard of us, ye received it not as the word of men, but as it is in truth, the word of God, which effectually worketh also in you that believe."

When ye received the word of God… ye received it not as the word of men, but as… the word of God. Was there a time before your salvation that you believed that the Bible was just another book? Or perhaps like me, you were taught as a little child that the Bible was God's Word. But there came a time when you realized that this truly is GOD'S WORD, written by men as breathed to them by God Himself. Thank you, Lord, for the enlightened knowledge that the Scriptures are your Word, and in them are the Words of salvation and life!

_____
_____
_____
_____
_____

Daily Reading: Joshua 7-9

March 6

1 Chronicles 17:20 "O LORD, there is none like thee, neither is there any God beside thee, according to all that we have heard with our ears."

O LORD, there is none like thee. When you explore other religions, you discover that the gods of those religions are man-made. Man does not have the ability to create a true god. Our God is an all-powerful and merciful God, THE GOD who made us, who loves us and cares for us as a Father, and who provides eternal life with Him, in the glories of Heaven. Thank you, Lord, for being that kind of God, One who holds me in His hand, who hears and answers prayer! There is none like You!

Daily Reading: Joshua 10-12

March 7

2 Samuel 22:31 "As for God, his way is perfect; the word of the LORD is tried: he is a buckler to all them that trust in him."

He is a buckler to all them that trust in him. A buckler is a circular shield—a protection in time of war or attack. Aren't you thankful that you have this protection? Those who love the Lord are being attacked by Satan every day. Thank you, Lord, that you are my Shield and my Buckler, protecting me daily from Satan, who seeks to devour me!

_____
_____
_____
_____
_____
_____
_____
_____

Daily Reading: Joshua 13-15

March 8

1 Peter 4:14 "If ye be reproached for the name of Christ, happy are ye; for the spirit of glory and of God resteth upon you: on their part he is evil spoken of, but on your part he is glorified."

If ye be reproached for the name of Christ, happy are ye. The Lord said that we would be persecuted for His name's sake. In my younger years, I suffered little persecution, as a weak Christian. I am happy that Satan's minions now see Christ in me enough that they want to squelch my witness. Thank you, Lord, that through Jesus I am a threat to Satan's purpose, that You shine in my life even to the wicked of this world!

Daily Reading: Joshua 16-18

March 9

Psalm 68:6 "God setteth the solitary in families: he bringeth out those which are bound with chains: but the rebellious dwell in a dry land."

God setteth the solitary in families. Being from a large family, it is difficult for me to imagine one not having family love and support, but there are many who have no one. When you accept Jesus and salvation, you become a part of the Family of God—now THAT is a large family! When you are baptized, you become a member of that local assembly of believers. Thank you, Lord, for providing a family for anyone who believes, and a local assembly where I may go for that yearned-for love and support!

Daily Reading: Joshua 19-21

March 10

Colossians 4:12 "Epaphras, who is one of you, a servant of Christ, saluteth you, always labouring fervently for you in prayers, that ye may stand perfect and complete in all the will of God."

Always labouring fervently for you in prayers. In Paul's letter to the Colossians, he tells them that Epaphras is always praying for their church at Colossae. Aren't you thankful for those who pray for you? In our church services, the men are called upon to pray, and many times, as the pastor's wife, I am mentioned in their prayer. I pray often for our church members, naming each in my prayer. Thank you, Lord, for this assembly and for all those who pray for my husband and for me!

_____
_____
_____
_____
_____
_____
_____

Daily Reading: Joshua 22-24

March 11

Psalm 81:7 "Thou calledst in trouble, and I delivered thee; I answered thee in the secret place of thunder: I proved thee at the waters of Meribah. Selah."

Thou calledst in trouble, and I delivered thee. God has delivered me many times when I have called out to him. I witness to others of God's goodness in helping me in times of trouble and heartache. Often those who do not profess to believe Jesus is Lord will ask me to pray when they are in times of crisis. Thank you, Lord, that You hear my prayers and that You deliver me, or You strengthen me in these times when I call upon You!

_____

_____

_____

_____

_____

_____

_____

Daily Reading: Judges 1-3

March 12

Galatians 3:8 "And the scripture, foreseeing that God would justify the heathen through faith, preached before the gospel unto Abraham, saying, In thee shall all nations be blessed."

God would justify the heathen through faith. God made His promise to Abraham, and later to Jacob (Israel), that he would bless His Chosen People. In that same promise to Abraham, He promised that ALL nations would be blessed in Abraham. The coming Savior would come as a descendent of Abraham, that all the world could partake of the blessing of salvation through faith in the Savior. Thank you, Lord, for your love and mercy, that a lowly sinner and Gentile such as I may have eternal life with You as my Savior and my Lord!

_____

_____

_____

_____

_____

_____

_____

Daily Reading: Judges 4-6

March 13

2 Samuel 22:29 "For thou art my lamp, O LORD: and the LORD will lighten my darkness."

The LORD will lighten my darkness. Before you came to Christ you were in the darkness of sin, but then the Gospel of God's Word was revealed to you, lighting the way of truth and salvation. Thank you, Lord, for that light, for giving me a sure and certain future of peace and joy with You!

_____
_____
_____
_____
_____
_____
_____
_____

Daily Reading: Judges 7-9

March 14

Deuteronomy 28:11 "And the LORD shall make thee plenteous in goods, in the fruit of thy body, and in the fruit of thy cattle, and in the fruit of thy ground, in the land which the LORD sware unto thy fathers to give thee."

The LORD shall make thee plenteous in goods. God promises His people plenty of goods, children, cattle, and crops. At times you may feel poor and needy, but when you consider all of God's blessings, you realize you are rich indeed. Thank you, Lord, for your abundant provisions!

_____

_____

_____

_____

_____

_____

_____

Daily Reading: Judges 10-12

March 15

1 Corinthians 2:9 "But as it is written, Eye hath not seen, nor ear heard, neither have entered into the heart of man, the things which God hath prepared for them that love him."

The things which God hath prepared for them that love him. When you consider all the blessings we have in this life, it is difficult to imagine that the next life will be even better. We cannot fathom what God has in store for those who love Him! Thank you, Lord, for the blessings of this life and for the many unimaginable things you have for me in my future!

_____

_____

_____

_____

_____

_____

_____

Daily Reading: Judges 13-15

March 16

Psalm 18:48 "He delivereth me from mine enemies: yea, thou liftest me up above those that rise up against me: thou hast delivered me from the violent man."

He delivereth me from mine enemies. As a Christian, you probably have enemies unknown, people who hate you because you love the Lord. Many of those enemies are violent people who would wish to do you physical harm, but God has protected you, either by keeping them from you, or by working in the enemy's mind to turn them from their intended evil against you. Thank you, Lord, for your watch care over me and over my loved ones!

___

Daily Reading: Judges 16-18

March 17

Luke 2:30-32 "For mine eyes have seen thy salvation, which thou hast prepared before the face of all people: a light to lighten the Gentiles, and the glory of thy people Israel."

A light to lighten the Gentiles. In the New Testament, God sent Paul to bring the light of His Word to the Gentile nations. Paul traveled over many countries, on three continents. Over the next two thousand years, the Word was shared by many and traveled to the rest of the world. In 1973, an elder soft-spoken pastor preached Jesus in words clear and plain, and the Spirit of God lightened me—and I was gloriously saved! Thank you, Lord, for sending first Paul, then others with the Gospel, and for saving my dark and sinful soul!

_____
_____
_____
_____
_____
_____
_____

Daily Reading: Judges 19-21

March 18

Psalm 71:5 "For thou art my hope, O Lord GOD: thou art my trust from my youth."

For thou art my hope. It is a sad thing to see persons who have no love, no hope, those who feel they have no reason to live. I once worked with a lady whom I pray for often. She told me that her sin was so bad that God could not forgive her. I explained to her that He will forgive anyone who comes to Him, believing and trusting in Him. She moved away and I have lost contact with her, but it continues to haunt me that she wanders in this world lost and with no hope. Thank you, Lord, that your Word was revealed to me, that my hope is in you!

_____

_____

_____

_____

_____

_____

_____

Daily Reading: Ruth 1-3

March 19

Psalm 48:14 "For this God is our God for ever and ever: he will be our guide even unto death."

He will be our guide even unto death. I have seen the peace that precedes that moment when a child of God takes his last breath. God is there with him, taking him into glory. All fear and pain are gone, as he is guided by the all-powerful, loving, and merciful God! Thank you, Lord, for your daily guidance, even into the hands of death!

Daily Reading: Ruth 4, 1 Samuel 1-3

March 20

Luke 2:11 "For unto you is born this day in the city of David a Saviour, which is Christ the Lord."

For unto you is born…a Saviour. Jesus, the Son of God, was born a man on this earth, to experience life as we know it, with trials, troubles, and temptations. He came UNTO US—to suffer and die for our sins. He left the throne of heaven, the beauty, the cleanness, the glories of heaven to live on this dark, dirty, nasty, sin-filled earth, with the purpose of paying the price for our sins—death on the cruel cross. Thank you, Jesus, for giving yourself, for suffering and dying for my sins, for paying the price that I could not pay!

___

___

___

___

___

___

___

Daily Reading: 1 Samuel 4-6

March 21

1 John 4:4 "Ye are of God, little children, and have overcome them: because greater is he that is in you, than he that is in the world."

Greater is he that is in you. At times we all feel weak and helpless. However, we have a source of strength to overcome sin and temptation, to keep us going when any action seems impossible. Like an energy drink to the soul, God gives us motivation and ability when our own power is insufficient. Thank you, Lord, for your greatness, strength, and power!

Daily Reading: 1 Samuel 7-9

March 22

1 Peter 1:23 *"Being born again, not of corruptible seed, but of incorruptible, by the word of God, which liveth and abideth for ever."*

Being born again, not of corruptible seed, but of incorruptible. When you are born again, you are saved forever by God's grace and power. This Scripture tells us we are born again of incorruptible seed, forever, never ending, never to be contaminated, never to die. God's grace provides for eternal life to every believer, a glorious and wonderful life in the presence of Jesus in Heaven! Thank you, Lord, for the promise of eternal security, forever saved, forever with Him!

_____

_____

_____

_____

_____

_____

Daily Reading: 1 Samuel 10-12

March 23

Acts 14:17 "Nevertheless he left not himself without witness, in that he did good, and gave us rain from heaven, and fruitful seasons, filling our hearts with food and gladness."

And gave us rain from heaven. In our lifetimes we sometimes have periods of drought, when the rain does not come for weeks, possibly months. We may feel God has forgotten us when we fail to see His hand in our lives, and we are blind to His blessings. But then the rains come! We see the abundant blessings mixed with His love and grace, giving us a feeling of gratefulness, a refreshing. Thank you, Lord, for those times of abundance of rain, when you pour out your blessings upon me!

_____
_____
_____
_____
_____
_____
_____

Daily Reading: 1 Samuel 13-15

March 24

Deuteronomy 28:9 "The LORD shall establish thee an holy people unto himself, as he hath sworn unto thee, if thou shalt keep the commandments of the LORD thy God, and walk in his ways."

The LORD shall establish thee an holy people unto himself. In the Old Testament, God chose the Israelites as His people. In the New Testament, and on into the present time, God's people are "whosoever will". Those who repent and confess Jesus as their Savior, and who live a life pleasing to Him are established as His holy people, a people set apart for His honor and glory. Thank you, Lord, for counting me in that number, a holy people!

Daily Reading: 1 Samuel 16-18

March 25

Psalm 23:1 "The LORD is my shepherd; I shall not want."

I shall not want. Probably the most quoted verse of Scripture, the twenty-third Psalm has many marvelous blessings that are often overlooked. Have you ever been in a situation of wanting something? Perhaps it was a material item, or a loved one's salvation or healing. We are to pray with faith. Then give thanks to the Lord for the thing for which we prayed, even before we receive it. What assurance we have that we shall not want. Thank you, Lord, that You provide our needs and wants!

_____
_____
_____
_____
_____
_____
_____

Daily Reading: 1 Samuel 19-21

March 26

Song of Solomon 2:4 "He brought me to the banqueting house, and his banner over me was love."

He brought me to the banqueting house. Don't you enjoy a banquet, with all the fellowship and wonderful selection of foods and beverages? The feast with Jesus in Heaven will be more magnificent, so sensational that we cannot imagine what it will be like—and the fellowship—with Jesus and the saints of old! Thank you, Lord, for the promises of a forever in the glories of Heaven!

_____

Daily Reading: 1 Samuel 22-24

March 27

Colossians 1:9a "For this cause we also, since the day we heard it, do not cease to pray for you..."

We do not cease to pray for you. As a pastor's wife, church members often pray for my husband and me. I am thankful for every one. I think that the private prayers for us greatly outnumber those spoken in public. I regularly pray for each member of our little congregation. How humbling it is to be remembered in prayer and to know that they are heard by the Creator of our universe. Thank you, Lord, for hearing our petitions!

Daily Reading: 1 Samuel 25-27

March 28

Hebrews 4:9 "There remaineth therefore a rest to the people of God."

A rest to the people of God. At times much work must be done, and we never seem to get enough rest. When we vacation, we tend to pack so much activity into the time, and though we enjoy ourselves, we still do not ease from our labors. Don't you look forward to a time away from your toils? That day is coming. Thank you, Lord, that a time of rest is coming for your people!

Daily Reading: 1 Samuel 28-31

March 29

Psalm 51:7 "Purge me with hyssop, and I shall be clean: wash me, and I shall be whiter than snow."

I shall be clean. We have all had garments that have been ruined with stain when we have spilled something that will not wash out. We too are stained with sin. And no matter what we do, we cannot remove that disgrace of sin by ourselves—not with works, not with kindness, not with generosity, not with repeat prayer and sacrifice. Only the mercy and grace of Jesus can cleanse us. Thank you, Lord, for the shedding of blood, and for your wonderful love, mercy and grace that saves and cleanses me from every stain of sin!

Daily Reading: 2 Samuel 1-3

March 30

John 15:14 "Ye are my friends, if ye do whatsoever I command you."

Ye are my friends. It is great to have friends; someone you can talk with and who you can count on in times of trouble. But friends often fail, perhaps sharing a confidence you wanted kept secret, failing to provide comfort when you are hurting or support when you need it. Your Friend Jesus never fails. He is there for you to share your secrets, to guide you, to comfort you and to support you in times of need. Thank you, Jesus, for always being there; thank you for being my Friend!

_____
_____
_____
_____
_____
_____
_____

Daily Reading: 2 Samuel 4-6

March 31

John 9:25 "He answered and said, Whether he be a sinner or no, I know not: one thing I know, that, whereas I was blind, now I see."

I was blind, now I see. The blind man was healed of his physical blindness by Jesus. Before our salvation, our eyes were blinded by Satan, and we could not see the goodness of God. But from the day we believed, our eyes were opened, and we see daily the blessed workings of the Lord, in nature, in people's lives, in all the world. Thank you, Lord, for opening my eyes, for healing my spiritual blindness!

Daily Reading: 2 Samuel 7-9

April 1

John 14:27 "Peace I leave with you, my peace I give unto you: not as the world giveth, give I unto you. Let not your heart be troubled, neither let it be afraid."

My peace I give unto you. At times you may feel that your life is total chaos. Perhaps you have lost your job, are having family troubles, maybe sickness or death of a loved one. Regardless of what is happening in your life, lean upon Jesus for peace. Thank you, Lord, for that peace that passes all understanding!

Daily Reading: 2 Samuel 10-12

April 2

Psalm 47:8 "God reigneth over the heathen: God sitteth upon the throne of his holiness."

God reigneth over the heathen. When Scripture speaks of the heathen, it speaks of Gentiles, which includes all people who are not Jewish. In other words, God reigns over all people of the world. He reigns over all His creation. What a wonderful God we serve! Thank you, Lord, for your power and majesty!

Daily Reading: 2 Samuel 13-15

April 3

Hebrews 10:17 "And their sins and iniquities will I remember no more."

Their sins... will I remember no more. When we think on our sins of the past, some things haunt us, and we just cannot forget. But God remembers them no more. They are gone, washed away with the blood of Jesus when we first believed and trusted Him as Savior. Thank you, Lord, that you do not see my sins, that they are no longer in your remembrance!

Daily Reading: 2 Samuel 16-18

April 4

Isaiah 26:4 "Trust ye in the LORD for ever: for in the LORD JEHOVAH is everlasting strength."

In the Lord is everlasting strength. At times we feel strong and confident, but then there are times the Lord reminds us that we are weak and helpless without Him. He provides the strength we need when we look to Him and call upon Him. Thank you, Lord, for your power, and for your reminders that I need your strength!

_____

_____

_____

_____

_____

_____

_____

Daily Reading: 2 Samuel 19-21

April 5

1 John 5:3 "For this is the love of God, that we keep his commandments: and his commandments are not grievous."

His commandments are not grievous. God gave us rules to live by, and over the years, we find that those commandments are not burdensome, but rules for a stress free and happy life. Sin always brings with it guilt, worry and anxiety, and often more sin. If we would only obey! Thank you, Lord, for the guide to a pleasant, carefree life!

Daily Reading: 2 Samuel 22-24

April 6

Jude 1:24 "Now unto him that is able to keep you from falling, and to present you faultless before the presence of his glory with exceeding joy."

Present you faultless. In our physical bodies we know that we lack perfection. However, when we die and stand before God, we will be presented by Christ faultless—perfect, sinless, unblemished, because Jesus died for our sins. He took the punishment for them all. Thank you, Lord, for taking on my sins, that I may be perfect and righteous before my Father!

Daily Reading: 1 Kings 1-3

April 7

Job 5:17 "Behold, happy is the man whom God correcteth: therefore despise not thou the chastening of the Almighty."

Happy is the man whom God correcteth. No child is happy when undergoing correction from his father. Discipline is for his good, to make him a better person. As a child reaches adulthood, or becomes a parent, he comes to the realization that correction was because of his father's love for him. Thank you, Lord, for your chastisement, for that is proof of your love for me!

_____
_____
_____
_____
_____
_____
_____

Daily Reading: 1 Kings 4-6

April 8

2 Thessalonians 3:3 "But the Lord is faithful, who shall stablish you, and keep you from evil."

The Lord *will* keep you from evil. As time progresses, the world becomes more and more wicked. The daily news is a depiction of evil against mankind. God protects us, His children from much of the viciousness in this world. Thank you, Lord, for your faithfulness and protection!

_____
_____
_____
_____
_____
_____
_____

Daily Reading: 1 Kings 7-9

April 9

Psalm 78:38 "But he, being full of compassion, forgave their iniquity, and destroyed them not: yea, many a time turned he his anger away, and did not stir up all his wrath."

But he forgave their iniquity, and destroyed them not. God has shown His mercy time and again in Scripture when the Israelites turned away from Him to worship idols. He forgave their sins when they came to Him in repentance, just as He forgives ours, when we turn back to Him. Thank you, Lord, for being faithful to forgive my sins and transgressions!

_____

_____

_____

_____

_____

_____

_____

Daily Reading: 1 Kings 10-12

April 10

Psalm 78:39 "For he remembered that they were but flesh; a wind that passeth away, and cometh not again."

He remembered that they were but flesh. God, our Creator, is perfect in all His ways. When He looks upon us, with our sins and shortcomings, He remembers that we are just flesh. In His great mercy and grace, He provides an escape from the coming judgment, if we will trust and believe in Jesus. Thank you, Lord, for remembering that I am but flesh, sinful and wicked, in need of a Savior, in need of your mercy!

Daily Reading: 1 Kings 13-15

April 11

Revelation 21:23 "And the city had no need of the sun, neither of the moon, to shine in it: for the glory of God did lighten it, and the Lamb is the light thereof."

And the city had no need of the sun. Scientists tell us that eventually the sun will burn out and life on our planet earth will die. In the story of creation, God created the light on the first day, but did not create the sun and moon until the fourth day. Jesus is the light, and when this earth has been destroyed, and the sun is no more, we will have the light of Jesus to illuminate our way. Thank you, Lord, for being my Light!

_____

_____

_____

_____

_____

_____

_____

Daily Reading: 1 Kings 16-18

April 12

John 14:19 "Yet a little while, and the world seeth me no more; but ye see me: because I live, ye shall live also."

Because I live, ye shall live also. Our earthly bodies are doomed to die. However, we have the promise of life eternal if we know Jesus as our Savior. At death, the saved person simply changes location, from this wicked earth, filled with sorrow and trouble, to the glories of Heaven, with Jesus. Thank you, Lord, that you overcame death, so that I shall live forever with you!

Daily Reading: 1 Kings 19-22

April 13

Jeremiah 15:16 "Thy words were found, and I did eat them; and thy word was unto me the joy and rejoicing of mine heart: for I am called by thy name, O LORD God of hosts."

I am called by thy name. Are you a Christian? The word Christian means "Christ-like". What a privilege to be called by the name of my Savior and God, Jesus **Christ**. He died for my sin, and lives and reigns forever. Thank you, Lord, that I am Christian, called by your blessed name!

_____

_____

_____

_____

_____

_____

_____

Daily Reading: 2 Kings 1-3

April 14

John 11:40 "Jesus saith unto her, Said I not unto thee, that, if thou wouldest believe, thou shouldest see the glory of God?"

Thou shouldest see the glory of God. To see the glory of God is no small thing. God said that if we would look upon His face in this life we would die (Exodus 33:20). After we die, we will see God, in all His glory. Thank you, Lord, that I will see you, my King and my Lord, the One who saved my soul!

_____

_____

_____

_____

_____

_____

_____

Daily Reading: 2 Kings 4-6

April 15

1 Thessalonians 2:13 "For this cause also thank we God without ceasing, because, when ye received the word of God which ye heard of us, ye received it not as the word of men, but as it is in truth, the word of God, which effectually worketh also in you that believe."

The word of God, which effectually worketh also in you that believe. The Word of God works in you, through the power of the Holy Spirit, giving you the ability to believe and receive salvation offered by grace through faith. Thank you, Lord, for the quickening of the Holy Spirit that resulted in my salvation!

Daily Reading: 2 Kings 7-9

April 16

Psalm 90:1 "LORD, thou hast been our dwelling place in all generations."

Thou hast been our dwelling place. The Hebrew word for dwelling place in this Scripture is *ma'own*, the word for retreat or asylum. We have a shelter in the Lord from our trials and troubles, from temptation and sin, through all generations, forever. Thank you, Lord, for this protection, my dwelling place with you!

_____
_____
_____
_____
_____
_____
_____

Daily Reading: 2 Kings 10-12

April 17

Ecclesiastes 7:3 "Sorrow is better than laughter: for by the sadness of the countenance the heart is made better."

By the sadness of the countenance the heart is made better. We have all experienced times of a heavy heart. This Scripture tells us that these experiences make our hearts better. Our pain and suffering make us more empathetic and sympathetic to the trials and sorrows of others. Without rainy days, would we appreciate the sunshine? Thank you, Lord, for the hard times, that I may be tender toward those facing misery and pain!

Daily Reading: 2 Kings 13-15

April 18

Philippians 1:21 "For to me to live is Christ, and to die is gain."

To die is gain. Many people fear death. To those who are saved, death is a promotion from this life of trials and troubles to a wonderful eternity of sharing the glories of Heaven in the presence of Jesus. A forever vacation with no parting, no pain, no sickness, no death. Thank you, Lord, for this glorious hope and promise of the home you have prepared for me!

Daily Reading: 2 Kings 16-18

April 19

Psalm 40:17 "But I am poor and needy; yet the Lord thinketh upon me: thou art my help and my deliverer; make no tarrying, O my God."

The Lord thinketh upon me. It gives you a feeling of importance to be recognized by the CEO of a large company, or a high government official. God, the Creator of the universe, thinks on you—YOU are highly regarded! Thank you, Lord, for having me in your thoughts, and for saving my soul!

Daily Reading: 2 Kings 19-21

April 20

1 Peter 2:15 "For so is the will of God, that with well doing ye may put to silence the ignorance of foolish men."

Ye may put to silence the ignorance of foolish men. Sometimes I shake my head at the foolishness of some individuals. People scoff at God's Words of warning, they continue in their sinful ways, and often ridicule those standing for God's truths. One day, they will be silenced. Thank you, Lord, for the wisdom of your Word, and for lighting the way for me!

Daily Reading: 2 Kings 22-25

April 21

Psalm 68:19 "Blessed be the Lord, who daily loadeth us with benefits, even the God of our salvation. Selah."

Loadeth us with benefits. A benefit is something that enhances our day or our life. Think on the many benefits we have: sunshine, a warm home, family and friends, good food, the beauties of song, nature, even color and smell—all things that give us pleasure. And we are LOADED with benefits. Thank you, Lord, for the many good things you provide me every day!

_____

_____

_____

_____

_____

_____

_____

Daily Reading: 1 Chronicles 1-4

April 22

Philippians 3:10 "That I may know him, and the power of his resurrection, and the fellowship of his sufferings, being made conformable unto his death."

The power of his resurrection. Consider the power it required to resurrect from the dead as Jesus did. No human on earth has this power, the power must come from God. Jesus has that power, as He alone is God and man. He resurrected Himself, and He will take us from the grave as well. Thank you, Lord, for the power you possess over death!

_____
_____
_____
_____
_____
_____
_____

Daily Reading: 1 Chronicles 5-7

April 23

Isaiah 66:18 "For I know their works and their thoughts: it shall come, that I will gather all nations and tongues; and they shall come, and see my glory."

I will gather all nations and tongues. In all the history of the world, there have been few days when there were no wars and fighting. The news is filled with it. People are mean and hateful, despising and hurting those of other nations and races. The day is coming when all will be gathered as one. Only God can bring that to be, as man is proud and sinful. Thank you, Lord, that the day is coming when I will be among that one people, one race, worshipping and praising you!

Daily Reading: 1 Chronicles 8-10

April 24

Luke 21:33 "Heaven and earth shall pass away: but my words shall not pass away."

My words shall not pass away. Reading Scripture can take away all your fears and anxiety, knowing that God is in control of every situation. God's Word has survived through thousands of years, even though many wicked men have vowed to destroy every Bible, every Scripture. Thank you, Lord, that your Word has endured, and will continue to exist forever!

_____
_____
_____
_____
_____
_____
_____

Daily Reading: 1 Chronicles 11-13

April 25

Amos 4:13 "For, lo, he that formeth the mountains, and createth the wind, and declareth unto man what is his thought, that maketh the morning darkness, and treadeth upon the high places of the earth, The LORD, The God of hosts, is his name."

He... declareth unto man what is his thought. The Word of God tells man of God's thoughts. Just as we share our ideas and aspirations with those we love, God does the same for us in His Word. What a blessing to know the mind and heart of God! Thank you, Lord, for sharing your ideas and judgments!

_____

_____

_____

_____

_____

_____

Daily Reading: 1 Chronicles 14-16

April 26

Psalm 98:1 "O sing unto the LORD a new song; for he hath done marvelous things: his right hand, and his holy arm, hath gotten him the victory."

He hath done marvelous things. When you study science, you get a glimpse of some of the marvelous works God has done. It is amazing to consider the science of genetics, how two cells come together to grow and develop into a live human being. And not only did God create the universe, He made a way for man to enter the glories of Heaven. Thank you, Lord, for all the marvelous things you have done!

_____
_____
_____
_____
_____
_____
_____

Daily Reading: 1 Chronicles 17-19

April 27

2 Timothy 1:11 "Whereunto I am appointed a preacher, and an apostle, and a teacher of the Gentiles."

I am appointed…a teacher of the Gentiles. Paul was one of the first missionaries who traveled over a huge geographic area, with the job of sharing the Word of God with the Gentiles. After Paul, God appointed many more through the years with the same assignment—take the Gospel to the lost Gentiles. Thank you, Lord, for the preacher who brought your Word to me, that I might come to know your saving grace!

_____
_____
_____
_____
_____
_____
_____

Daily Reading: 1 Chronicles 20-23

April 28

Nehemiah 2:18 "Then I told them of the hand of my God which was good upon me; as also the king's words that he had spoken unto me. And they said, Let us rise up and build. So they strengthened their hands for this good work."

The hand of my God which was good upon me. Nehemiah had the hand of God upon him, giving him the support of the people to build the wall around Jerusalem. Whether your work is to write, to teach, to preach or just to give a helping hand to someone in need, it is good when God's hand is upon you to do it. Thank you, Lord, for your hand guiding me to do the work you would have me to do!

Daily Reading: 1 Chronicles 24-26

April 29

Psalm 9:8 "And he shall judge the world in righteousness, he shall minister judgment to the people in uprightness."

He shall judge the world in righteousness. Nearly every day there is a news story of a judge who has been bribed or who conspired to give an unjust verdict or decision. God's judgments are always just and right. He has no respect of persons. He will punish all sin. Some sin was judged at Calvary, for those who believe and trust Jesus as Savior. The sin of those who have rejected Jesus will be punished in the eternal fires of hell. Thank you, Lord, for your righteous judgment, and for saving me from that eternal punishment!

Daily Reading: 1 Chronicles 27-29

April 30

1 John 4:18 "There is no fear in love; but perfect love casteth out fear: because fear hath torment. He that feareth is not made perfect in love."

There is no fear in love. It is not perfect love when one lives in dread of rejection or loss of that love. With the love of Christ, we have no worry of rejection, of His change of heart, of loss of His love. Christians have a perfect love and are forever in Christ. Thank you, Lord, for that eternal security without doubt or fear!

_____
_____
_____
_____
_____
_____
_____

Daily Reading: 2 Chronicles 1-3

May 1

Psalm 50:15 "And call upon me in the day of trouble: I will deliver thee, and thou shalt glorify me."

I will deliver thee. At times we go through trials and troubles, hurts and heartache—be it death of a loved one, serious illness, financial troubles, etc. No matter what the hardship may be, if we call upon the Lord, He will deliver us. That is His promise. Thank you, Lord, for the many times you have delivered me, and for the future times that are yet to come!

_____
_____
_____
_____
_____
_____
_____
_____

Daily Reading: 2 Chronicles 4-6

May 2

Hebrews 6:10 "For God is not unrighteous to forget your work and labour of love, which ye have shewed toward his name, in that ye have ministered to the saints, and do minister."

God *will not* forget your work and labour of love. How many times have you done something for someone and have received no thanks or appreciation? And then at times good works you have done are unseen by all, except by God. He appreciates all that is done as a labor of love, and He will not forget it. Thank you, Lord, that you remember the good works I do, as your appreciation of one task means more to me than a thousand from men!

_____
_____
_____
_____
_____
_____
_____

Daily Reading: 2 Chronicles 7-9

May 3

Exodus 15:2 "The LORD is my strength and song, and he is become my salvation: he is my God, and I will prepare him an habitation; my father's God, and I will exalt him."

The Lord is my strength. At times we feel we cannot go on and we become so burdened that we feel like quitting. Then the Lord provides strength for the battle. With His encouragement and might we can be steadfast and ready to meet whatever is before us. Thank you, Lord, for your strength, might, and power, for without you I can do nothing!

_____

_____

_____

_____

_____

_____

_____

Daily Reading: 2 Chronicles 10-12

May 4

3 John 1:4 "I have no greater joy than to hear that my children walk in truth."

My children walk in truth. Nothing quite stirs the soul like the moment your child professes Jesus as Savior—that is a parent's daily prayer. This Scripture, written by John the apostle, refers to those he has led to Christ, not children by birth. As a Sunday School teacher of young people, knowing that a child I taught has been saved and is living a life pleasing to God brings me great joy. Thank you, Lord, for those who have come to know you through my teaching or influence! May they ever give you glory and praise!

Daily Reading: 2 Chronicles 13-15

May 5

Genesis 5:1b "In the day that God created man, in the likeness of God made he him."

In the likeness of God made he him. Knowing that we are made in the likeness of God should prompt us to try to be more like Him, just as a child tries to be like his parent. God, who is the all-powerful, all-knowing, eternal, and mighty God, Creator of all, has made **US** in His likeness. Thank you, Lord, for creating me in your image. Help me daily to be more like you!

_____

_____

_____

_____

_____

_____

_____

Daily Reading: 2 Chronicles 16-18

May 6

Psalm 146:7 "Which executeth judgment for the oppressed: which giveth food to the hungry. The LORD looseth the prisoners."

The Lord looseth the prisoners. Many high government officials have the authority to pardon prisoners at their choosing, regardless of the verdict and sentence that had been imposed upon them. Jesus has a much greater authority. We are guilty of sin, and the sentence for that sin is forever in the pits of hell. But Jesus goes before His Father, telling Him that He has pardoned the sinner who trusts and believes in Him. Thank you, Lord, for this pardon, for your love, mercy and grace that has freed me!

Daily Reading: 2 Chronicles 19-21

May 7

Acts 20:24a "But none of these things move me, neither count I my life dear unto myself, so that I might finish my course with joy..."

Neither count I my life dear unto myself. Many people endure hardships and even death in order to take the Gospel to others that souls may be saved. Of the disciples who were present at Pentecost, most died a martyr's death. Still today, many face severe persecution and death for spreading the Word of God. Without these brave individuals, we may not have ever heard the Word or known the joy of salvation. Thank you, Lord, for those who have not counted their lives dear, who have suffered and died that sinners like me may be saved!

_____
_____
_____
_____
_____
_____
_____

Daily Reading: 2 Chronicles 22-24

May 8

1 John 5:18b "… he that is begotten of God keepeth himself, and that wicked one toucheth him not."

That wicked one toucheth him not. When we reach Heaven, we will come to know many things that are not revealed to us on this earth. We will see the times that God protected us from the hands of Satan and his demons. As a child of God, He shields us from that wicked one who would like nothing better than to devour us. Thank you, Lord, for your care and defense, for I do not have power against Satan without you!

___
___
___
___
___
___
___

Daily Reading: 2 Chronicles 25-27

May 9

Psalm 5:3 "My voice shalt thou hear in the morning, O LORD; in the morning will I direct my prayer unto thee, and will look up."

My voice shalt thou hear. God hears us when we call upon Him, in the morning or any time of day. He is ready to hear our praises and petitions at any time we choose. Do you have a special time of day to go to Him in prayer? He is waiting and listening. Thank you, Lord, for giving your attention to my every prayer!

Daily Reading: 2 Chronicles 28-30

May 10

Hebrews 10:12 "But this man, after he had offered one sacrifice for sins for ever, sat down on the right hand of God."

He had offered one sacrifice for sins for ever. Jesus died on Calvary and Scripture tells us that His death was a sacrifice that was sufficient payment for all sins. There is no more need for sacrifice, Jesus paid it ALL. Thank you, Lord, for going to the cross, for suffering the punishment for my sins!

_____
_____
_____
_____
_____
_____
_____

Daily Reading: 2 Chronicles 31-33

May 11

Romans 8:1 "There is therefore now no condemnation to them which are in Christ Jesus, who walk not after the flesh, but after the Spirit."

There is therefore now no condemnation. As children of Adam, we are born with a sinful nature, condemned to die. But God gave His Son, that we might be pardoned, that we may live. Jesus took upon Himself the punishment for our sin, that we may escape that curse of death. Thank you, Jesus, for dying for me, that I have been freed from that condemnation!

Daily Reading: 2 Chronicles 34-36

May 12

Malachi 3:10b "...prove me now herewith, saith the LORD of hosts, if I will not open you the windows of heaven, and pour you out a blessing, that there shall not be room enough to receive it."

Pour you out a blessing, that there shall not be room enough to receive it. When the Lord answers prayer, or provides you a blessing, He always gives much more than what you ask or expect. Abraham prayed for a son and God provided him a son, but also gave him descendants more numerous than the stars. God opens the windows of heaven and pours out His bounty. Thank you, Lord, for the many favors you have provided me, for I am not worthy!

Daily Reading: Ezra 1-3

May 13

Psalm 133:1 "Behold, how good and how pleasant it is for brethren to dwell together in unity!"

How pleasant it is for brethren to dwell together in unity! Don't you love church homecomings, Bible conferences, and revival services? Gathering with other Christians gives an awesome glimpse of what it will be like in Heaven. King David experienced this same joy. Thank you, Lord, for those times of unity, of meeting with others to bring you praise and glory!

Daily Reading: Ezra 4-7

May 14

1 Thessalonians 2:7 "But we were gentle among you, even as a nurse cherisheth her children."

We were gentle among you. Many of us are not naturally gentle and caring. God changes our hearts when we come to Him for salvation, and then we become more like Jesus, loving and kindhearted, particularly toward the lost. That compassion leads us to share the grace and mercy of God and compels men to preach and to go to mission works. Thank you, Lord, for giving me a heart that wants to reach others for you!

_____
_____
_____
_____
_____
_____
_____
_____

Daily Reading: Ezra 8-10

May 15

Psalm 139:14 "I will praise thee; for I am fearfully and wonderfully made: marvelous are thy works; and that my soul knoweth right well."

I am fearfully and wonderfully made. The workings of the human body are amazing. Consider any one of the systems of the human body: the circulatory system that moves blood to other organs, providing nutrition and life; the eye that focuses, working with the brain to process what the eye sees. We truly are wonderfully made. Thank you, Lord, for creating me with intelligence and for creating me in your image!

_____

_____

_____

_____

_____

_____

Daily Reading: Nehemiah 1-4

May 16

Matthew 5:11-12 "Blessed are ye, when men shall revile you, and persecute you, and shall say all manner of evil against you falsely, for my sake… for great is your reward in heaven…"

Blessed are ye, when men shall revile you. When you live a Christian life, sometimes people around you simply will not like you. They may do things in an attempt to harm your testimony, even telling lies about you. But Scripture says that this is a blessing, for you will be rewarded in Heaven. Thank you, Lord, that my life shines for you enough that the devil's people want to harm me, for that I will be rewarded!

_____
_____
_____
_____
_____
_____
_____

Daily Reading: Nehemiah 5-7

May 17

Isaiah 25:1 "O LORD, thou art my God; I will exalt thee, I will praise thy name; for thou hast done wonderful things; thy counsels of old are faithfulness and truth."

Thy counsels of old are faithfulness and truth. People will let you down, will break their promises, will lie to you. Spouses are unfaithful, parents make promises they cannot keep, friends gossip behind your back, etc. However, you can always rely on God's truth and His promises—for the one thing God cannot do is lie (Titus 1:2). Thank you, Lord, that your Word never fails, that you are honest and true, and FAITHFUL!

_____

_____

_____

_____

_____

_____

_____

Daily Reading: Nehemiah 8-10

May 18

Proverbs 17:6 "Children's children are the crown of old men; and the glory of children are their fathers."

Children's children are the crown of old men. Having children is a blessing and thrill, but grandchildren are all of that multiplied. If you have not experienced the delight of children and grandchildren, perhaps the Lord has blessed you with delightful children in your family, church, or neighborhood. Thank you, Lord, for my children and grandchildren, and for all of those children you have sent my way!

_____

_____

_____

_____

_____

_____

_____

Daily Reading: Nehemiah 11-13

May 19

Psalm 73:23 "Nevertheless I am continually with thee: thou hast holden me by my right hand."

Thou hast holden me by my right hand. Being from a family of eight children, I rarely went shopping or on vacation as a child. When I did, my parent or an older sibling would hold my hand, giving me a feeling of security and safety. God holds us by the hand, that we have freedom from danger and fear. Thank you, Lord, for your protection, for holding my hand!

Daily Reading: Esther 1-3

May 20

1 Timothy 4:15 "Meditate upon these things; give thyself wholly to them; that thy profiting may appear to all."

Thy profiting may appear to all. When we spend much time in prayer and in studying God's Word we develop to become more like Jesus. This Scripture tells us that this growth will be apparent to others around us. This may result in two things: the lost will want what we have and the saved are encouraged in the Lord. Thank you, Lord, for the time I have to study and to pray!

___
___
___
___
___
___
___

Daily Reading: Esther 4-6

May 21

Philippians 4:19 "But my God shall supply all your need according to his riches in glory by Christ Jesus."

But my God shall supply all your need. Physically, we need nothing more than food, water, shelter, and clothing. However, humans have other needs. We have a need to socialize with others, and we have a need to know God. We need salvation. God will provide every need if we just seek Him. Thank you, Lord, for providing for all my needs, particularly the need of salvation!

___
___
___
___
___
___
___

Daily Reading: Esther 7-10

May 22

Psalm 138:6 "Though the LORD be high, yet hath he respect unto the lowly: but the proud he knoweth afar off."

Though the Lord be high, yet hath he respect unto the lowly. Some people who are wealthy and powerful do not give the time of day to the average person, whom they do not consider to be on the same level. God is the Maker of all, the Creator, the Lord. Yet He regards lowly sinners, who deserve nothing. He considers our needs and our wants, He loves us, and provides a Savior for whosoever will believe. Thank you, Lord, for your care and love, for I am simple, common, and unworthy!

Daily Reading: Job 1-3

May 23

Revelation 1:11a "Saying, I am Alpha and Omega, the first and the last: and What thou seest, write in a book..."

What thou seest, write in a book. God has given us sixty-six books that tell of Jesus our Savior. They instruct us how to live a successful life and give us a glimpse of the future. The Book of Revelation is a book of the beauties of Heaven and the prophesy of the end times. Each time I read through Revelation I discover some new mystery revealed. Thank you, Lord, for the Holy Bible, for in it are the Words of Life!

Daily Reading: Job 4-6

May 24

Deuteronomy 28:10 "And all people of the earth shall see that thou art called by the name of the LORD; and they shall be afraid of thee."

Thou art called by the name of the Lord; and they shall be afraid of thee. This was one of the many blessings from the Lord to Israel, God's chosen people. Word spread throughout the world in those times that God fought for Israel. When they went against other nations, the people of other lands trembled and often fled, knowing they had no chance against Israel's powerful God. God fights for Christians as well when we live for Him and obey His Word. Thank you, Lord, for your power and might, and for contending for your people!

_____
_____
_____
_____
_____
_____
_____
_____

Daily Reading: Job 7-9

May 25

Philippians 1:3 "I thank my God upon every remembrance of you."

Every remembrance of you. Think on the memories of your Christian sisters and brothers. I love to reminiscence about the sweet pastor who told me about Jesus, who was concerned for my salvation. I cherish the recollection of the elder ladies who shared their blessings and wisdom when I was a young Christian, wife, and mother. Thank you, Lord, for these remembrances and for the joy they still provide me!

Daily Reading: Job 10-12

May 26

Psalm 66:20 "Blessed be God, which hath not turned away my prayer, nor his mercy from me."

Blessed be God, which hath not turned away my prayer. Do you keep record of answered prayers? I would have volumes had I written down every answered prayer. When we go to God with our petitions and with a pure heart, He hears our every prayer. Thank you, Lord, for hearing my supplications and for all answered prayers!

_____

_____

_____

_____

_____

_____

_____

Daily Reading: Job 13-15

May 27

1 John 5:20 "And we know that the Son of God is come, and hath given us an understanding, that we may know him that is true, and we are in him that is true, even in his Son Jesus Christ. This is the true God, and eternal life."

The Son of God is come, and hath given us an understanding, that we may know him. We come to know God through His Son, Jesus, who became man. He revealed His Godly attributes in miracles and His resurrection. He became man that we may know God and enjoy the glories of Heaven. Thank you, Lord, that I may know God through you and through your life and your Word!

Daily Reading: Job 16-18

May 28

Psalm 46:10 "Be still, and know that I am God: I will be exalted among the heathen, I will be exalted in the earth."

Be still, and know that I am God. This verse is often quoted, but do we really think of just what it is saying? We tend to go day to day, trying to live our lives in our own strength and intelligence. When we run into problems, that is when we must stop and BE STILL—let God take the wheel. He can handle all those trials that overwhelm us. Thank you, Lord, for your strength and power that will overcome whatever comes my way!

Daily Reading: Job 19-21

May 29

John 10:27 "My sheep hear my voice, and I know them, and they follow me."

My sheep hear my voice, and I know them. Jesus knows His sheep. He knows those of us who are His. Jesus is the Great Shepherd, who guides and guards His sheep. He protects us from predators and other dangers, He guides us in the way we should go. Thank you, Lord, for your safekeeping and for your direction and instruction that keeps me from straying from your fold!

_____
_____
_____
_____
_____
_____
_____

Daily Reading: Job 22-24

May 30

John 10:28 *"And I give unto them eternal life; and they shall never perish, neither shall any man pluck them out of my hand."*

And I give unto them eternal life; and they shall never perish. When we accept Jesus as Savior, He gives us salvation, eternal life that will never change. He knows we have not the power to keep ourselves. Through the power of His resurrection He secures us forever. Thank you, Lord, for your wonderful grace and mercy, and for the promise of eternal life in you!

Daily Reading: Job 25-27

May 31

John 10:29 "My Father, which gave them me, is greater than all; and no man is able to pluck them out of my Father's hand."

No man is able to pluck them out of my Father's hand. This is an assurance of the permanence of our salvation. The word *man* in this verse and in the previous verse is italicized indicating that the word was added to make the sentence understandable. No man, no power, NOTHING, can pluck us from God's hand. Thank you, Lord, for your power that saves me and keeps me forever as yours!

Daily Reading: Job 28-30

June 1

Matthew 13:23 "But he that received seed into the good ground is he that heareth the word, and understandeth it; which also beareth fruit, and bringeth forth, some an hundredfold, some sixty, some thirty."

He that received seed...beareth fruit. How much fruit are you bearing in your life since you came to know Jesus? Share the love of Jesus with those you meet. Live a life that tells others that you are His. Bring your fruits to the Master, show Him with your gifts your love and thankfulness to Him. Thank you, Lord, that I have fruits acceptable to you for you alone are worthy!

___

___

___

___

___

___

___

Daily Reading: Job 31-33

June 2

Psalm 147:3 "He healeth the broken in heart, and bindeth up their wounds."

He healeth the broken in heart. When you have been betrayed by one you love, one thing will bring healing and comfort—the joy of knowing the One who never lies, who is always faithful—Jesus. He is steadfast and true, the source of healing. Thank you, Lord, for your love and care, for the times you have restored my broken heart!

_____
_____
_____
_____
_____
_____
_____

Daily Reading: Job 34-36

June 3

Acts 13:47 "For so hath the Lord commanded us, saying, I have set thee to be a light of the Gentiles, that thou shouldest be for salvation unto the ends of the earth."

I have set thee to be a light of the Gentiles. God called Paul to be a missionary to the Gentiles. He traveled over all the world as he knew it, he shared the Gospel, organized churches, and encouraged Christians who were saved under his ministry. Over the years, churches have sent out other missionaries to do the same and God's Word has been taken to the whole world. Thank you, Lord, for those who share your love and mercy to those in my country and in far-away lands!

Daily Reading: Job 37-39

June 4

2 Timothy 1:3 *"I thank God, whom I serve from my forefathers with pure conscience, that without ceasing I have remembrance of thee in my prayers night and day."*

I have remembrance of thee in my prayers night and day. Often when I pray, names are brought to my mind. Many are people whom I have never met but have heard of their need of the Lord's intercession. What a blessing when I hear that my prayers have been answered. Thank you, Lord, for hearing my prayers, for your help and healing for those in need!

_____

_____

_____

_____

_____

_____

_____

Daily Reading: Job 40-42

June 5

Psalm 32:7 "Thou art my hiding place; thou shalt preserve me from trouble; thou shalt compass me about with songs of deliverance. Selah."

Thou art my hiding place. We all have times when we feel the need to just hide away from the cares and trials of the day. God provides that hiding place. Go to Him in prayer and spend time in His Word. A retreat with the Lord will restore your strength and your joy. Thank you, Lord, for the hiding place I have with you!

Daily Reading: Psalm 1-5

June 6

1Peter 1:3-4 "Blessed be the God and Father of our Lord Jesus Christ, which according to his abundant mercy hath begotten us again unto a lively hope by the resurrection of Jesus Christ from the dead, to an inheritance incorruptible, and undefiled, and that fadeth not away, reserved in heaven for you."

An inheritance incorruptible, and undefiled. When Joshua led the Israelites into the Promised Land, he gave each of the families a section of land, their inheritance. We have an inheritance coming, one that is incorruptible, that will never end, a legacy in Heaven, according to our promise from God. Thank you, Lord, for your promise of a home forever in Heaven!

_____
_____
_____
_____
_____
_____

Daily Reading: Psalm 6-10

June 7

John 8:58 "Jesus said unto them, Verily, verily, I say unto you, Before Abraham was, I am."

Before Abraham was, I am. Jesus was speaking to a group of Jews, who questioned Him when He spoke of Abraham. They could not understand how Jesus, not yet fifty years old, could have seen Abraham. Jesus' answer told them that He always was, He had no beginning, because He was God Himself. Thank you, Lord, for your Son Jesus, who had no beginning, and has no end!

Daily Reading: Psalm 11-15

June 8

Proverbs 6:23 "For the commandment is a lamp; and the law is light; and reproofs of instruction are the way of life."

The commandment is a lamp; and the law is light. The commandments given by God give us direction of how we should live our lives, but most of all, they shed light on the fact that we cannot live a sinless life. Since we sin, we need a Savior, because no sin may enter Heaven. Thank you, Lord, that you showed me my sin, and my need of you, and that you have forgiven every sin!

_____
_____
_____
_____
_____
_____
_____

Daily Reading: Psalm 16-20

June 9

Psalm 59:16 "But I will sing of thy power; yea, I will sing aloud of thy mercy in the morning: for thou hast been my defence and refuge in the day of my trouble."

Thou hast been my defence and refuge in the day of my trouble. In your days of trouble, where do you go? Do you moan and complain, do you work harder and fiercer, or do you go to the Lord, who is your defense and refuge? In Isaiah 41:10 God says, "I will help thee." Depend upon Him and make your life simple and painless. Thank you, Lord, for being my Protector and my Shield!

_____
_____
_____
_____
_____
_____
_____

Daily Reading: Psalm 21-25

June 10

John 17:9 "I pray for them: I pray not for the world, but for them which thou hast given me; for they are thine."

I pray for them… which thou hast given me. In this Scripture, Jesus is speaking. He prayed for ME, for YOU, for all the saved. At times, if you feel unimportant or unloved, return to this verse. Every soul that is saved was given to Jesus by Father God, and Jesus prayed for each one, and later died for them. That is love! Thank you, Lord, for your prayers and intercession for me, a lowly sinner!

_____

_____

_____

_____

_____

_____

Daily Reading: Psalm 26-30

June 11

Genesis 1:31 "And God saw every thing that he had made, and, behold, it was very good. And the evening and the morning were the sixth day."

Behold, it was very good. When God created the earth and all that was in it, it was all good. However, man's sin brought corruption, decay, and death to God's unblemished creation. Even though much of it is tainted with man's touch, there is much beauty in nature for us to enjoy. Thank you, Lord, for the loveliness that remains in your creation!

_____
_____
_____
_____
_____
_____
_____

Daily Reading: Psalm 31-35

June 12

1 Timothy 4:4 "For every creature of God is good, and nothing to be refused, if it be received with thanksgiving."

Every creature of God is good, and nothing to be refused. Under Jewish law, certain foods were declared clean and unclean, and the unclean were not to be eaten by man. New Testament scripture did away with dietary restrictions in Acts 10:15, confirmed in the above verse. We have a huge variety of foods to choose from, making eating a pleasant experience. Thank you, Lord, for the various foods I have and enjoy!

_____
_____
_____
_____
_____
_____
_____

Daily Reading: Psalm 36-40

June 13

Psalm 119:98 "Thou through thy commandments hast made me wiser than mine enemies: for they are ever with me."

Thou...hast made me wiser than mine enemies. When we spend time reading and studying God's Word, He blesses us with wisdom from the Bible, giving us dominance over our enemies. Often, our response to an adversary brings us victory when we do not counter their actions with hate and venom but respond with love and patience. Strength and power are found in God's Word. Thank you, Lord, for the Scriptures and for the advantage you provide me in the knowledge of your Word!

Daily Reading: Psalm 41-45

June 14

Jude 1:14b-15 "Behold, the Lord cometh with ten thousands of his saints, to execute judgment upon all, and to convince all that are ungodly among them of all their ungodly deeds which they have ungodly committed, and of all their hard speeches which ungodly sinners have spoken against him."

The Lord cometh with ten thousands of his saints, to execute judgment. The ungodly are becoming more accepted in this wicked world: in government, in entertainment, in business and in all aspects of today's society. A day of judgment is coming when the ungodly sinners will be convinced of their sinful ways before the Great White Throne of Judgment. Thank you, Lord, that you convinced me of my sin before the judgment, leading me to Jesus, my Savior, and to your mercy and grace!

Daily Reading: Psalm 46-50

June 15

Colossians 3:10 "And have put on the new man, which is renewed in knowledge after the image of him that created him."

And have put on the new man. When one is saved, he is made new, the old man dies. The temptations remain, but the desire to please God is greater. The new man is being renewed daily, continually developed into the image of the Savior, becoming more and more like Jesus. Thank you, Lord, for making me new, for giving me a desire to be like you!

Daily Reading: Psalm 51-55

June 16

Exodus 15:11 "Who is like unto thee, O LORD, among the gods? Who is like thee, glorious in holiness, fearful in praises, doing wonders?"

Who is like thee... doing wonders? Nothing and no one can compare to God. None are like Him. His works are glorious and marvelous. He has created all the worlds. He has sent His Son Jesus as a Savior to all who will believe. He has worked in the hearts of all who are His. Thank you, Lord, for your wonderful works!

___

___

___

___

___

___

___

Daily Reading: Psalm 56-60

June 17

Psalm 34:4 "I sought the LORD, and he heard me, and delivered me from all my fears."

He heard me, and delivered me from all my fears. What do you fear—wickedness, war, sickness, unemployment, harm or death? The Lord will deliver you from all of that and more, giving you a peace that passes our understanding. Even through the difficult and trying times, He is with you if you call upon Him. Thank you, Lord, for deliverance and redemption—I will not fear because you are with me!

___
___
___
___
___
___
___

Daily Reading: Psalm 61-66

June 18

Ephesians 1:11 "In whom also we have obtained an inheritance, being predestinated according to the purpose of him who worketh all things after the counsel of his own will."

In whom also we have obtained an inheritance. Have you ever been the recipient of an inheritance? Perhaps you inherited thousands of dollars of worth, perhaps millions or more. Whatever you may have received will be as rubble when compared to the eternal inheritance and the riches of Heaven that we will receive as a child of God. Thank you, Lord, for the birthright I possess as your child!

_____
_____
_____
_____
_____
_____
_____

Daily Reading: Psalm 67-71

June 19

2 Peter 1:4 "Whereby are given unto us exceeding great and precious promises: that by these ye might be partakers of the divine nature, having escaped the corruption that is in the world through lust."

Ye might be partakers of the divine nature, having escaped the corruption that is in the world. All that is in the world will one day rot and decompose or be burned and destroyed. Of our works, only that which is for the Lord will escape annihilation. Thank you, Lord, for showing me the momentary pleasure received from worldly possessions, and the eternal reward obtained in you!

Daily Reading: Psalm 72-76

June 20

Psalm 67:4 "O let the nations be glad and sing for joy: for thou shalt judge the people righteously, and govern the nations upon the earth. Selah."

Thou shalt judge the people righteously, and govern the nations upon the earth. In the daily news, we read of cheating and bribery, unjust decisions and actions that are taken to satisfy greed and the yearning for power. When Christ returns, He will govern. He will be the perfect ruler and judge. Thank you, Lord, for that coming day, when you will be the righteous King of all the earth and Heaven!

_____

_____

_____

_____

_____

_____

_____

Daily Reading: Psalm 77-80

June 21

Ephesians 2:13 "But now in Christ Jesus ye who sometimes were far off are made nigh by the blood of Christ."

Ye who sometimes were far off are made nigh by the blood of Christ. In Old Testament times the Jewish people were said to be nigh, or near, because they had access to God through the temple. Gentiles were "far off", with no admission to the temple. Before our salvation we were far off, with no admittance to the throne of God. Through Christ's blood we are brought nigh, we have a passage to God. Thank you, Lord, for bringing me nigh unto you, that I may have access to your love, mercy, and grace!

Daily Reading: Psalm 81-85

June 22

Leviticus 20:7 "Sanctify yourselves therefore, and be ye holy: for I am the LORD your God."

Be ye holy: for I am the Lord your God. Without Christ, we have no holiness, we are sinful and desperately wicked. With Jesus as our Savior, we begin the process of sanctification, as we draw closer to the Lord through prayer and reading His Word. Thank you, Lord, that I may be holy—for YOU!

_____

_____

_____

_____

_____

_____

_____

Daily Reading: Psalm 86-90

June 23

Proverbs 18:10 "The name of the LORD is a strong tower: the righteous runneth into it, and is safe."

The name of the Lord is a strong tower. When we get into situations of trouble and fear, we need only to call upon the name of Jesus for strength and safety. He is our strong tower, our place of refuge. Thank you, Lord, for the security and protection I find in you!

_____
_____
_____
_____
_____
_____
_____
_____

Daily Reading: Psalm 91-96

June 24

Genesis 8:1 "And God remembered Noah, and every living thing, and all the cattle that was with him in the ark: and God made a wind to pass over the earth, and the waters asswaged."

And God remembered Noah, and every living thing. The Bible says that before God sent the flood upon the earth that the earth was corrupt and filled with violence. But Noah found grace in the eyes of the Lord. Just as God remembered Noah, God will remember His people who love and serve Him. Thank you, Lord, for remembering me, for providing me your grace and mercy!

Daily Reading: Psalm 97-100

June 25

Galatians 3:14 "That the blessing of Abraham might come on the Gentiles through Jesus Christ; that we might receive the promise of the Spirit through faith."

The blessing of Abraham might come on the Gentiles. Through Abraham, the Israelites, God's Chosen People were promised blessings. God never forgot His promises even though His people often turned from Him and sinned greatly. After Jesus came to this earth God's blessings were expanded to include the Gentiles. His promise of the Spirit through faith is the free gift of salvation. Thank you, Lord, for saving me, for the Holy Spirit that works in me!

Daily Reading: Psalm 101-105

June 26

Psalm 89:18 "For the LORD is our defence; and the Holy One of Israel is our king."

For the Lord is our defence. When going before Goliath the giant, David said, "This day will the LORD deliver thee into mine hand; and I will smite thee…" (1 Samuel 17:46). All throughout his life, David knew the power and protection of God. He is the Defender against spiritual as well as physical powers. Thank you, Lord, for your care and safekeeping in my life!

_____
_____
_____
_____
_____
_____
_____

Daily Reading: Psalm 106-109

June 27

Psalm 63:5 "My soul shall be satisfied as with marrow and fatness; and my mouth shall praise thee with joyful lips."

My soul shall be satisfied. People spend their lives seeking satisfaction—in riches, in power, in love, in lust, in knowledge. These may bring temporary pleasure, but lifelong satisfaction is found only in Jesus. He alone can satisfy your soul. Seek Him, find Him, and serve Him, and you will find pleasure and fulfillment. Thank you, Lord, for the satisfaction I have found in you!

Daily Reading: Psalm 110-115

June 28

2 John 1:9 "Whosoever transgresseth, and abideth not in the doctrine of Christ, hath not God. He that abideth in the doctrine of Christ, he hath both the Father and the Son."

He that abideth in the doctrine of Christ, he hath both the Father and the Son. The doctrine of Christ is that He is the only Son of God, sent to save the world. If one believes this and lives for Jesus, he has both God the Son, Jesus, and God the Father. This is possible through God the Holy Spirit. Thank you, Lord, that I have the Father, the Son, and the Holy Spirit, that they live in me, and I live in them!

_____

_____

_____

_____

_____

_____

_____

Daily Reading: Psalm 116-118

June 29

James 1:5 "If any of you lack wisdom, let him ask of God, that giveth to all men liberally, and upbraideth not; and it shall be given him."

If any of you lack wisdom, let him ask of God… and it shall be given him. Many people think of themselves as wise. However, this world's wisdom is foolishness with God. True wisdom is from God, from His Word. God is the Creator of all, the source of all wisdom. Thank you, Lord, for your wisdom, and your Word, wherein is true understanding and knowledge!

_____

_____

_____

_____

_____

_____

_____

Daily Reading: Psalm 119:1-88

June 30

Joshua 8:35 "There was not a word of all that Moses commanded, which Joshua read not before all the congregation of Israel, with the women, and the little ones, and the strangers that were conversant among them."

There was not a word of all that Moses commanded, which Joshua read not before all the congregation. As a child of God, we are responsible to read and study the Word, that we may know God's truths. If you are being taught the whole counsel of God by your pastor, you are blessed. Thank you, Lord, for preachers who have taught me your truths from your Word!

Daily Reading: Psalm 119:89-176

July 1

2 Chronicles 7:14 *"If my people, which are called by my name, shall humble themselves, and pray, and seek my face, and turn from their wicked ways; then will I hear from heaven, and will forgive their sin, and will heal their land."*

Then I will hear from heaven, and will forgive their sin. Time and again in the Old Testament, the children of Israel turned from God and worshipped idols. And over and over they cried out to God for pardon and for relief from His judgments. God is faithful and just to forgive when His people repent of their wickedness. Thank you, Lord, that you are a God of goodness and mercy and that you repeatedly have forgiven my sins!

Daily Reading: Psalm 120-124

July 2

John 14:16 "And I will pray the Father, and he shall give you another Comforter, that he may abide with you forever."

He shall give you another Comforter, that he may abide with you forever. When Jesus drew near the time of His death, He began to prepare His disciples for when He would no longer walk among them. While He was with them, they drew strength knowing of Jesus' power, but after He died, they became fearful and apprehensive. Jesus promised another Comforter, the Holy Spirit, who came upon them on the day of Pentecost, giving them boldness and courage. Thank you, Lord, for your Holy Spirit that dwells in me, for with your Spirit, I have no fear!

Daily Reading: Psalm 125-129

July 3

Psalm 125:2 "As the mountains are round about Jerusalem, so the Lord is round about his people from henceforth even for ever."

The Lord is round about his people from henceforth even for ever. God promised in both the Old and New Testaments to forever be with His people, and history has proved that to be true. God's people have been tormented and tried, but later, God blessed them abundantly for their faithfulness. Thank you, Lord, for always being with me and for your promise of never leaving me!

_____
_____
_____
_____
_____
_____
_____

Daily Reading: Psalm 130-135

July 4

Leviticus 25:10a "And ye shall hallow the fiftieth year, and proclaim liberty throughout all the land unto all the inhabitants thereof..."

Proclaim liberty throughout all the land unto all the inhabitants thereof. This is the inscription on the liberty bell, the bell that was made in 1751 to mark the fiftieth anniversary of William Penn's Charter of Privileges. The liberty bell has been a symbol of independence for the United States for over 200 years, and until it cracked, was often rang to mark patriotic events in our history. When we accept the free gift of salvation, we have declared our independence from sin and eternal death. Thank you, Lord, for freeing me from the clutches of Satan!

Daily Reading: Psalm 136-140

July 5

Galatians 5:16 "This I say then, Walk in the Spirit, and ye shall not fulfil the lust of the flesh."

Walk in the Spirit, and ye shall not fulfil the lust of the flesh. When we are saved and we walk with God each day, we have the power to overcome our fleshly desires and do right according to God's Word. The things of this life lose their enticement when we concentrate on God's Word and our salvation, making temptations easier to overcome. Thank you, Lord, for the blessings of life in you, that make my desire to please you in all things!

_____
_____
_____
_____
_____
_____
_____

Daily Reading: Psalm 141-144

July 6

Ephesians 1:3 "Blessed be the God and Father of our Lord Jesus Christ, who hath blessed us with all spiritual blessings in heavenly places in Christ."

Blessed be the God... who hath blessed us with all spiritual blessings. When we consider our blessings from the Lord, often we look at our physical blessings, such as family, home, food and clothing, good health, etc. But when we think on our spiritual blessings, oh, what a wonder! We have eternal salvation, God's love, peace, power, strength, and a certain future. Thank you, Lord, for your bountiful blessings and for your promise of my eternity in the glories of Heaven!

___

___

___

___

___

___

___

Daily Reading: Psalm 145-147

July 7

Psalm 34:22 "The LORD redeemeth the soul of his servants: and none of them that trust in him shall be desolate."

None of them that trust in him shall be desolate. When you witness the desolation and hopelessness of the lost sinner you see a sad sight, when tomorrow brings nothing but a repeat of the troubles and sorrows of today. However, when a sinner is saved, he has a glorious transition. When one trusts and believes in Jesus, nothing today can bring him down and regardless of what happens tomorrow, God is with him through it all. Thank you, Lord, for your redemption, and for giving me a beautiful today and a bright tomorrow!

Daily Reading: Psalm 148-150

July 8

Isaiah 51:11 "Therefore the redeemed of the LORD shall return, and come with singing unto Zion; and everlasting joy shall be upon their head: they shall obtain gladness and joy; and sorrow and mourning shall flee away."

Sorrow and mourning shall flee away. We experience many sorrows in this world. Loved ones go through horrible tribulations, some are gravely ill, some die. However, the day is coming when all grief and heartbreak will be no more for the saved in Christ. Thank you, Lord, for the coming day, when I will live eternally in your presence, experiencing all joy and wonder, praising and worshiping you!

Daily Reading: Proverbs 1-4

July 9

Psalm 37:23 "The steps of a good man are ordered by the LORD: and he delighteth in his way."

The steps of a good man are ordered by the Lord. The world has turned from God, and many call evil good and good evil. How is a man to know what is right? The Bible is our guidebook, with instruction for every aspect of life, if we will just search its truths. When we live for Christ, the Holy Spirit guides us in all that we do. Thank you, Lord, for guiding me and leading me to do your will!

_____
_____
_____
_____
_____
_____
_____
_____

Daily Reading: Proverbs 5-7

July 10

1 Thessalonians 4:16 "For the Lord himself shall descend from heaven with a shout, with the voice of the archangel, and with the trump of God: and the dead in Christ shall rise first."

And the dead in Christ shall rise first. When Christ returns to take His people home to Heaven, He will first call those who are in the grave. They will come out of the graves to join Jesus, for their eternity in Heaven, where they will ever live with the Lord. Thank you, Lord, that if I die on this earth, that you will one day call me from my grave, and I will joyfully live forever with you!

Daily Reading: Proverbs 8-10

July 11

1 Thessalonians 4:17 "Then we which are alive and remain shall be caught up together with them in the clouds, to meet the Lord in the air: and so shall we ever be with the Lord."

Then we which are alive and remain shall be caught up together with them in the clouds. When Christ returns He will first call from the graves those saved who have died, then He will call those saved and alive on this earth to join them, and from that point we will be together with the Lord forever. Thank you, Lord, for saving me and that one day I will live eternally with you!

_____
_____
_____
_____
_____
_____
_____
_____

Daily Reading: Proverbs 11-13

July 12

Isaiah 41:10 "Fear thou not; for I am with thee: be not dismayed; for I am thy God: I will strengthen thee; yea, I will help thee; yea, I will uphold thee with the right hand of my righteousness."

I will strengthen thee; yea I will help thee. As Christians living and working in the world, we often feel alone and downtrodden. We do not fit in with the world, and at times, are shunned by those around us. But God gave Israel this promise, and He will do the same for all who live for Him—He will give us strength and help during those times. Thank you, Lord, for your support and might; I pray that you may continue to provide your power that I may always please you!

Daily Reading: Proverbs 14-16

July 13

Galatians 4:6-7 "And because ye are sons, God hath sent forth the Spirit of his Son into your hearts, crying, Abba, Father. Wherefore thou art no more a servant, but a son; and if a son, then an heir of God through Christ."

Thou art no more a servant, but a son... an heir of God through Christ. These two verses give us a hint of what we have as saved children of God: no more a servant or slave to sin, sons of God, heirs of God through Christ. God, the Maker and the One who owns all of creation—we, as His children, are His beneficiary! Thank you, Lord, that I am promised an estate, a legacy of yours. What blessings and riches you have bestowed upon me!

Daily Reading: Proverbs 17-19

July 14

Revelation 3:19 "As many as I love, I rebuke and chasten: be zealous therefore, and repent."

As many as I love, I rebuke and chasten. Correction meted out by a father is out of love for his child, and as a father would his sons and daughters, God punishes His children when they disobey Him. The punishment is not pleasant at the time, but when a Christian repents and turns from their sin, the relationship with God is restored. Thank you, Lord, for the times you have corrected me, and for your love, the love of the Father!

_____
_____
_____
_____
_____
_____
_____

Daily Reading: Proverbs 20-22

July 15

Psalm 34:10 "The young lions do lack, and suffer hunger: but they that seek the LORD shall not want any good thing."

They that seek the Lord shall not want any good thing. We who are Christians are so greatly blessed. God has promised us many wonderful blessings in this life and in the next. He fulfills our needs often before we ask. Thank you, Lord, for your abundant provision, for giving me all that I need!

_____
_____
_____
_____
_____
_____
_____

Daily Reading: Proverbs 23-25

July 16

Isaiah 66:20 "And they shall bring all your brethren for an offering unto the LORD out of all nations upon horses, and in chariots, and in litters, and upon mules, and upon swift beasts, to my holy mountain Jerusalem, saith the LORD, as the children of Israel bring an offering in a clean vessel into the house of the LORD."

And they shall bring all your brethren for an offering unto the Lord out of all nations. At the final judgment, God will call out all His people, from every nation throughout the world, both Jews and Gentiles. This chapter ends with the fearful prophesy of God's judgment upon the lost, and their devastating end in eternal hell fires. Thank you, Lord, for your saving love and mercy, that I will be among those called out, with those who will spend eternity with you!

___

___

___

___

___

Daily Reading: Proverbs 26-28

July 17

Genesis 9:11 "And I will establish my covenant with you; neither shall all flesh be cut off any more by the waters of a flood; neither shall there any more be a flood to destroy the earth."

Neither shall all flesh be cut off any more by the waters of a flood. After the great flood that destroyed all life on the earth except those on the ark with Noah, God promised never to destroy life in that manner again. Man was so horribly wicked that Scripture says, "It repented the LORD that he had made man". God did not make a mistake in creating man, but He was grieved by the sinfulness of His creation. Thank you, Lord, for this promise and for your longsuffering, as the world continues to be unrighteous and corrupt!

_____
_____
_____
_____
_____
_____
_____

Daily Reading: Proverbs 29-31

July 18

Psalm139:7-10 "Whither shall I go from thy spirit? Or whither shall I flee from thy presence? If I ascend up into heaven, thou art there: if I make my bed in hell, behold, thou art there. If I take the wings of the morning, and dwell in the uttermost parts of the sea; even there shall thy hand lead me, and thy right hand shall hold me."

Even there shall thy hand lead me, and thy right hand shall hold me. For a child of God, there is no place we can go where God is not with us. This is a comforting thought for those who are out of God's will and living in sin. Once we are saved by the shed blood of Jesus, there is nothing that can take us from God's hand. Thank you, Lord, for your eternal love and safekeeping!

___
___
___
___
___
___

Daily Reading: Ecclesiastes 1-3

July 19

Galatians 2:16 "Knowing that a man is not justified by the works of the law, but by the faith of Jesus Christ, even we have believed in Jesus Christ, that we might be justified by the faith of Christ, and not by the works of the law: for by the works of the law shall no flesh be justified."

Knowing that a man is not justified by the works of the law. Aren't you happy that your salvation is not based on your obedience to the law of God? We all are sinners, and any one sin will keep us from the glories of Heaven. But Christ justifies us when we believe He died to take away our sin. Thank you, Lord, for showing me the truths of your Word, that I am saved by grace through faith!

Daily Reading: Ecclesiastes 4-6

July 20

1 Corinthians 10:17 "For we being many are one bread, and one body: for we are all partakers of that one bread."

For we being many are one bread, and one body. When Scripture talks about the body, it speaks of the local, New Testament church, a local assembly of believers. There is great joy in congregating with fellow believers, meeting to worship and praise God, almost a glimpse of what it will be like in Heaven. Thank you, Lord, for establishing the church, for in it I have received great blessings!

_____
_____
_____
_____
_____
_____
_____

Daily Reading: Ecclesiastes 7-9

July 21

Psalm 108:13 "Through God we shall do valiantly: for he it is that shall tread down our enemies."

Through God we shall do valiantly. Most of us do not think of ourselves as being valiant, brave, or courageous. Those are not qualities that many of us possess in ourselves, but with God, we will tread down our enemies and we will overcome. Thank you, Lord, for the bravery and boldness I have in you!

_____
_____
_____
_____
_____
_____
_____
_____

Daily Reading: Ecclesiastes 10-12

July 22

Judges 6:10 "And I said unto you, I am the LORD your God; fear not the gods of the Amorites, in whose land ye dwell: but ye have not obeyed my voice."

Fear not the gods of the Amorites, in whose land ye dwell. The Midianites attacked Israel and destroyed all the foods, leaving nothing to eat for the people or the animals. God told Gideon this was the result of Israel's sin against Him. He reminded Gideon that if the people would turn back to Him, there was no need to fear. We have no reason to fear if we turn from our sin and repent. Thank you, Lord, that in you are blessings, power, and forgiveness!

_____
_____
_____
_____
_____
_____
_____

Daily Reading: Song of Solomon 1-4

July 23

Hebrews 2:9 "But we see Jesus, who was made a little lower than the angels for the suffering of death, crowned with glory and honour; that he by the grace of God should taste death for every man."

He by the grace of God should taste death for every man. Jesus came from the glories of Heaven to earth, walked among the people who rejected and ridiculed Him and suffered horrible death on the cross. He did that so that those who refused Him, those who mocked and taunted Him, those who killed Him, could be saved, if they just repented and turned to Him. Jesus willingly went to the cross, proving His great love for us. Thank you, Lord, that you came to this earth and paid the price for my sins!

Daily Reading: Song of Solomon 5-8

July 24

Matthew 12:39 "But he answered and said unto them, An evil and adulterous generation seeketh after a sign; and there shall no sign be given to it, but the sign of the prophet Jonas."

There shall no sign be given to it, but the sign of the prophet Jonas. The Pharisees came to Jesus, asking for a sign, and this was His response. Jonah spent three days in the belly of the great fish, just as Jesus would spend three days in the grave after His death. He would then return alive. Yet today, there are people seeking a sign, but what more do they need? Jesus died and rose again that man might be saved. Thank you, Lord, for dying for me and for saving me!

Daily Reading: Isaiah 1-3

July 25

Psalm 107:9 "For he satisfieth the longing soul, and filleth the hungry soul with goodness."

He satisfieth the longing soul. People seek satisfaction and happiness in fame, riches, power, love, and many other ways—always seeking, never finding. Fulfillment and true joy can only be found in the Lord. When one finds Jesus, the longing ends, and satisfaction is found. Thank you, Lord, for the joy I have in knowing you!

Daily Reading: Isaiah 4-6

July 26

Luke 9:56a "For the Son of man is not come to destroy men's lives, but to save them."

The Son of man is not come to destroy men's lives. Shortly before His death, when the Samaritans would not allow Jesus to stay in their village, James and John were livid and asked Jesus to destroy them. But Jesus responded that He came to save, not destroy. Jesus always returns love. Those who hate Him, who seek to destroy His Word and the testimony of His people, will be saved if they will turn to Him in faith and repentance. Thank you, Lord, for your great love for those whose sin is great, for at one time, that was me!

Daily Reading: Isaiah 7-9

July 27

Isaiah 12:2 "Behold, God is my salvation; I will trust, and not be afraid: for the LORD JEHOVAH is my strength and my song; he also is become my salvation."

Behold, God is my salvation. The Lord often reveals our human frailty. Amid a pandemic, we see that even for those who are young and strong, life hangs by a thread. When life on earth ends, each one goes before God for judgment. Those who trust and believe in Jesus as Savior will be rewarded for works done for His glory. Those who rejected Jesus will be banished to eternal fires of hell. Have you turned to Jesus in faith for forgiveness of your sins? Thank you, Lord, for giving me the free gift of salvation. I pray that all that I do will be to your glory!

Daily Reading: Isaiah 10-12

July 28

2 Peter 1:19 *"We have also a more sure word of prophecy; whereunto ye do well that ye take heed, as unto a light that shineth in a dark place, until the day dawn, and the day star arise in your hearts."*

A more sure word of prophesy... as unto a light that shineth in a dark place. All Scripture is written by the inspiration of God. These Words bring a blaze to the darkness, a ray of light and hope in this dark, sin-filled world. Thank you, Lord, for your illuminating Word, that showed me my sin, and my need of a Savior!

Daily Reading: Isaiah 13-15

July 29

Psalm 113:9 "He maketh the barren woman to keep house, and to be a joyful mother of children. Praise ye the LORD."

He maketh the barren woman… to be a joyful mother of children. Throughout Scripture we find accounts of several women who were infertile, who prayed to the Lord for a child. God granted that desire for some, and in the case of Hannah, God blessed with a number of children. Being a mother brings life-long joy. Thank you, Lord, for giving me the blessing of children and grandchildren!

Daily Reading: Isaiah 16-18

July 30

Luke 2:16-17 "And they came with haste, and found Mary, and Joseph, and the babe lying in a manger. And when they had seen it, they made known abroad the saying which was told them concerning this child."

They made known the saying which was told them concerning this child. This is a familiar part of the traditional Christmas story, when the shepherds came and saw the Baby Jesus. When they left, they made known what was told to them by the angel about this Baby—He is the Christ, the promised Savior! This has been proclaimed by Christians and preachers ever since. Thank you, Lord, for those who told me this joyful message, and for those who share it with others!

_____
_____
_____
_____
_____
_____

Daily Reading: Isaiah 19-21

July 31

Psalm 107:13 "Then they cried unto the LORD in their trouble, and he saved them out of their distresses."

He saved them out of their distresses. This Psalm is a celebratory song, praising God for delivering the Israelites out of Egypt, where they were enslaved and treated horribly. They called out to God, and He heard their cry. When we have troubles and distress, God hears us if we call on Him. Thank you, Lord, for the many times you heard my cry and delivered me and healed my heart!

_____
_____
_____
_____
_____
_____
_____

Daily Reading: Isaiah 22-24

August 1

Psalm 107:17, 19 "Fools because of their transgression, and because of their iniquities, are afflicted... Then they cry unto the LORD in their trouble, and he saveth them out of their distresses."

They cry unto the Lord in their trouble, and he saveth them out of their distresses. Often when we suffer distress and anxiety it is the result of our own sins— sins we have committed or the sin of not trusting the Lord. But blessings come from the knowledge that in our foolishness, if we cry to God, he will take us out of our worry and torment and forgive us. Thank you, Lord, for forgiving me the many times I have sinned and when I have not trusted in you to meet my needs!

Daily Reading: Isaiah 25-27

August 2

2 Corinthians 4:7 "But we have this treasure in earthen vessels, that the excellency of the power may be of God, and not of us."

We have this treasure in earthen vessels. Our physical bodies are our earthen vessels, weak and easily broken. But when we have Jesus, He dwells in us, giving us a power only He possesses. Through Him we can do all things. Thank you, Lord, for the power you have provided me in you!

_____

_____

_____

_____

_____

_____

_____

Daily Reading: Isaiah 28-30

August 3

1 John 4:16 "And we have known and believed the love that God hath to us. God is love; and he that dwelleth in love dwelleth in God, and God in him."

God is love; and he that dwelleth in love dwelleth in God, and God in him. Real and true love is only in the Lord. It is difficult for our little minds to grasp that when we are saved, that God dwells *in us*, and we live *in Him*, but this verse tells us it is so. That is a closeness to our Creator that just blows the mind. Thank you, Lord, for living in me, and that I live in you—what a beautiful relationship!

Daily Reading: Isaiah 31-33

August 4

Psalm 18:28 "For thou wilt light my candle: the LORD my God will enlighten my darkness."

The Lord my God will enlighten my darkness. When we are first saved, we may not know much about the Lord and His Word. We know that we are sinners and need a Savior. After salvation, we come to know more about God and His goodness and grace. When we hear the Word of God preached, when we study His Word, when we pray and He answers our prayers, every step lightens the darkness that we experienced and brightens our way. Thank you, Lord, for your light and your love!

_____

_____

_____

_____

_____

_____

_____

Daily Reading: Isaiah 34-36

August 5

2 Timothy 1:12b "… for I know whom I have believed, and am persuaded that he is able to keep that which I have committed unto him against that day."

He is able to keep that which I have committed unto him. When we are saved, we commit our lives to Jesus our Savior. From that point HE keeps us. If it were dependent upon us to keep ourselves saved, we likely would not last a full day. His powerful hand keeps us so that nothing can remove us from His saving grace. Thank you, Lord, for keeping me, for that assurance of eternal salvation in you!

_____

_____

_____

_____

_____

_____

Daily Reading: Isaiah 37-39

August 6

Psalm 50:3 "Our God shall come, and shall not keep silence: a fire shall devour before him, and it shall be very tempestuous round about him."

Our God shall come, and shall not keep silence. This verse tells of God's judgment, that it will be tempestuous, violent, and intense. But we know that God's judgment is just. He is God and the Creator of all. He gave His Son that man may escape this horrific judgment. Help me Lord to share your Word with the lost. Thank you, Lord, for your Son, for my salvation through Him!

Daily Reading: Isaiah 40-42

August 7

Luke 4:18 "The Spirit of the Lord is upon me, because he hath anointed me to preach the gospel to the poor; he hath sent me to heal the brokenhearted, to preach deliverance to the captives, and recovering of sight to the blind, to set at liberty them that are bruised."

He hath anointed me to preach the gospel to the poor. Jesus had returned to Nazareth to the town where He spent his childhood. He went to the temple on the Sabbath and opened the Scriptures to the Book of Isaiah and read to the people. Jesus was anointed or chosen to preach the Gospel—He was chosen to BE the Gospel, the Good News, that the promised Savior was here. Thank you, Lord, that you have opened the Scriptures to my blinded eyes that I may see the wonders of your salvation!

_____

_____

_____

_____

_____

_____

Daily Reading: Isaiah 43-45

August 8

Luke 4:18 "The Spirit of the Lord is upon me, because he hath anointed me to preach the gospel to the poor; he hath sent me to heal the brokenhearted, to preach deliverance to the captives, and recovering of sight to the blind, to set at liberty them that are bruised."

He hath sent me to heal the brokenhearted. If you have lived long enough you have experienced a broken heart. Perhaps from a love or marriage that failed, maybe one precious to you died, or some other tragedy occurred that resulted in grief or devastation. Healing is in the Lord. He can provide comfort unlike any other. Thank you, Lord, for being there when my heart was broken, for comforting me and holding me during those dark sad days!

_____

_____

_____

_____

_____

_____

Daily Reading: Isaiah 46-48

August 9

Luke 4:18 "The Spirit of the Lord is upon me, because he hath anointed me to preach the gospel to the poor; he hath sent me to heal the brokenhearted, to preach deliverance to the captives, and recovering of sight to the blind, to set at liberty them that are bruised."

He hath sent me... to preach deliverance to the captives. When we are lost, we are captives of sin and prisoners of Satan himself. In that condition we have no real joy and no hope. Jesus came to release us from the chains of sin and from the confines of Satan. Thank you, Lord, for pulling me from Satan's grasp, for delivering me from that horrible imprisonment!

Daily Reading: Isaiah 49-51

August 10

Luke 4:18 "The Spirit of the Lord is upon me, because he hath anointed me to preach the gospel to the poor; he hath sent me to heal the brokenhearted, to preach deliverance to the captives, and recovering of sight to the blind, to set at liberty them that are bruised."

He hath sent me to…recovering of sight to the blind. A lost person is blinded to God's love and to His hope in salvation. The Holy Spirit speaks through God's Word. He must open the eyes of the blind to see their sin and need of a Savior. (2 Corinthians 4:4) Thank you, Lord, for opening my sin-blinded eyes and for revealing to me the way of salvation!

Daily Reading: Isaiah 52-54

August 11

Luke 4:18 "The Spirit of the Lord is upon me, because he hath anointed me to preach the gospel to the poor; he hath sent me to heal the brokenhearted, to preach deliverance to the captives, and recovering of sight to the blind, to set at liberty them that are bruised."

He hath sent me...to set at liberty them that are bruised. Sin in our lives leaves a lasting mark. Even though that sin is erased when we repent and are saved, there remains a "bruise", the effects of sins of the past on our lives in this flesh. Those contusions will vanish when we leave this life and enter the glories of Heaven. Thank you, Lord, for those bruises, as they are a constant reminder of the sin from which you saved me!

Daily Reading: Isaiah 55-57

August 12

Romans 8:2 "For the law of the Spirit of life in Christ Jesus hath made me free from the law of sin and death."

Hath made me free from the law of sin and death. Those who believe they can get to Heaven through their works by trying to live a sinless life are doomed to the punishment of hell—for all have sinned and come short of the glory of God. When a person accepts Jesus as their Savior, by faith in His shed blood, he is freed from the law and promised an eternity in Heaven. Thank you, Lord, for the freedom I have in you, that I am no longer a slave to sin and the law!

Daily Reading: Isaiah 58-60

August 13

Psalm 36:5 "Thy mercy, O LORD, is in the heavens; and thy faithfulness reacheth unto the clouds."

Thy faithfulness reacheth unto the clouds. Friends and loved ones may be there to help you in times of need, but none is as faithful as Jesus. He is a true and loving Friend who will never leave you nor forsake you. Great is His faithfulness! Thank you, Lord, that through the years you have always been faithful, a dear friend who has never let me down!

_____
_____
_____
_____
_____
_____
_____

Daily Reading: Isaiah 61-63

August 14

Psalm 130:3-4 "If thou, LORD, shouldst mark iniquities, O Lord, who shall stand? But there is forgiveness with thee, that thou mayest be feared."

If thou... shouldst mark iniquities, O Lord, who shall stand? If we had to stand before God and be judged on our goodness and works, we all would fail to meet the standard to enter Heaven. Our sins would bring judgment from a just and powerful God. But there is forgiveness! When we repent and trust Jesus our sins are gone. Thank you, Lord, that through Jesus I am justified and my sins are forgiven!

_____

_____

_____

_____

_____

_____

_____

Daily Reading: Isaiah 64-66

A YEAR OF THANKSGIVING

August 15

Isaiah 14:24 "The LORD of hosts hath sworn, saying, Surely as I have thought, so shall it come to pass; and as I have purposed, so shall it stand."

As I have purposed, so shall it stand. Throughout the Bible we read of many prophesies, some that have already come to be and many that tell of future events. Those revelations will come to pass. What God has determined will come to be. Thank you, Lord, that my future is with you, and that your prophesies are certain!

_____

_____

_____

_____

_____

_____

Daily Reading: Jeremiah 1-3

August 16

Acts 11:18 "When they heard these things, they held their peace, and glorified God, saying, Then hath God also to the Gentiles granted repentance unto life."

Then hath God also to the Gentiles granted repentance unto life. A Gentile is anyone who is not a Jew (Israelite). After the Israelites sinned against God, He opened salvation to all. Whosoever comes to Jesus in repentance and faith shall be saved. Thank you, Lord, for saving me, for providing salvation to ALL who believe!

_____

_____

_____

_____

_____

_____

_____

Daily Reading: Jeremiah 4-6

August 17

Acts 13:29-30 "And when they had fulfilled all that was written of him, they took him down from the tree, and laid him in a sepulchre. But God raised him from the dead."

But God raised him from the dead. Many false gods are worshipped throughout the world, several of whom were men who walked on this earth as Jesus did. All these men died. Jesus was the only one who came back to life, who rose from the dead—proof that He is the Son of the One True God. Thank you, Lord, for your death, burial, and resurrection—for that is my hope that I will again live with you in Heaven!

_____

_____

_____

_____

_____

_____

_____

Daily Reading: Jeremiah 7-9

August 18

Genesis 9:13 "I do set my bow in the cloud, and it shall be for a token of a covenant between me and the earth."

It shall be for a token of a covenant between me and the earth. God destroyed the earth with the great flood. When the waters had gone down and Noah came out of the ark, God placed a rainbow in the sky. This was a sign of His promise that He would never again destroy the whole earth with water. When we see a rainbow, we can be assured of all of God's promises, for God cannot lie (Titus 1:2). Thank you, Lord, for your promises, for they are my hope!

_____

_____

_____

_____

_____

_____

_____

Daily Reading: Jeremiah 10-12

August 19

Psalm 93:4 "The LORD on high is mightier than the noise of many waters, yea, than the mighty waves of the sea."

The Lord on high is mightier... than the mighty waves of the sea. Man, in all his perceived wisdom and strength, has tried to control the waves of the sea. To date, there are tsunamis and storm surges that still destroy man and the works of men's hands. The waves of the ocean are strong and forceful, but God is more powerful. Thank you, Lord, that you have might greater than any known to man! You are my God and you hold me in your strong and stalwart hand!

_____
_____
_____
_____
_____
_____
_____

Daily Reading: Jeremiah 13-15

August 20

Ephesians 2:10 "For we are his workmanship, created in Christ Jesus unto good works, which God hath before ordained that we should walk in them."

We are his workmanship, created in Christ Jesus unto good works. We often hear of people who are said to be "self-made", usually people who are successful in the eyes of the world. To be successful, our lives must center on Christ. He makes us what we can be. We are precious in His eyes when we turn our lives over to His control. Thank you, Lord, for shaping me for your honor and glory!

Daily Reading: Jeremiah 16-18

August 21

Exodus 15:13 "Thou in thy mercy hast led forth the people which thou hast redeemed: thou hast guided them in thy strength unto thy holy habitation."

Thou in thy mercy hast led forth the people which thou hast redeemed. When we are saved, we are led by God until the time that we depart this life, when we will enter Heaven, His holy habitation. At times we are led astray by Satan or by our own will, but God will direct us back in the way we should go. Thank you, Lord, for guiding me along my way on this earth, and for the day you will lead me to my eternal home in glory!

_____

_____

_____

_____

_____

_____

_____

Daily Reading: Jeremiah 19-21

August 22

1 Peter 3:12 "For the eyes of the Lord are over the righteous, and his ears are open unto their prayers: but the face of the Lord is against them that do evil."

For the eyes of the Lord are over the righteous, and his ears are open unto their prayers. I have often wished that I had kept record of all my prayers that God has answered. They would fill volumes. God answers prayer. He tells us to ask and we shall receive. Thank you, Lord, for answered prayer, for your love, protection, healing, and guidance!

_____
_____
_____
_____
_____
_____
_____
_____

Daily Reading: Jeremiah 22-25

August 23

1 John 3:2 "Beloved, now are we the sons of God, and it doth not yet appear what we shall be: but we know that, when he shall appear, we shall be like him; for we shall see him as he is."

We shall be like him. Jesus is the perfect Son of God: sinless, full of love, forgiving. In Christ we will one day be like Him. When we appear before God in the judgment, we will appear sinless, as the blood of Jesus has washed away all our sin. As we walk this earth, we should try to be like Him, full of love and compassion, forgiving and reaching out to others whom we can help. Thank you, Lord, that I will one day be like you!

Daily Reading: Jeremiah 26-28

August 24

Psalm 46:1 "God is our refuge and strength, a very present help in trouble."

God is...a very present help in trouble. We live in troubling times. The world is full of wickedness, wars, disease, and natural disasters. But we have a refuge. God is our help in times of distress and difficulty. He is our Rock and our Strength. Thank you, Lord, for your care and protection, that I may have peace even in these troubled times!

Daily Reading: Jeremiah 29-31

August 25

Hebrews 12:1 "Wherefore seeing we also are compassed about with so great a cloud of witnesses, let us lay aside every weight, and the sin which doth so easily beset us, and let us run with patience the race that is set before us."

Wherefore seeing we also are compassed about with so great a cloud of witnesses. As we run the race of life, we are told that we are cheered on by that great cloud of witnesses, the saints who have gone before us. Therefore, we should rid ourselves of sin and endure with persistence till the end. Nothing stirs an athlete to carry on like the cheers of spectators. Thank you, Lord, for those who have gone on before, who have been my teachers and my cheerleaders!

Daily Reading: Jeremiah 32-34

August 26

2 Timothy 3:16 "All scripture is given by inspiration of God, and is profitable for doctrine, for reproof, for correction, for instruction in righteousness."

All scripture is given... for instruction in righteousness. The Scriptures not only show us the way of salvation, but also provide clear instructions for living for Christ. We have the law of the Old Testament as well as the example of Jesus in the New Testament. If we follow these, we will live a life pleasing and acceptable to God. Thank you, Lord, for your Word, that provides me with direction for my life, that I may live for you!

Daily Reading: Jeremiah 35-37

August 27

Psalm 18:2 "The LORD is my rock, and my fortress, and my deliverer; my God, my strength, in whom I will trust; my buckler, and the horn of my salvation, and my high tower."

The Lord is my... fortress... and my high tower. As we fight the war against sin, we have a great and strong defense with God. The fortress about us prevents the entering in of sin to destroy us and the high tower lets us see the coming enemy, that we may fight him off as he approaches. Thank you, Lord, for your strength and protection from my enemy, Satan!

Daily Reading: Jeremiah 38-40

August 28

Psalm 19:1 "The heavens declare the glory of God; and the firmament sheweth his handywork."

The heavens declare the glory of God. Scripture tells us that nature itself declares that God is our Creator. Consider our solar system, and how the earth rotates around the sun. The seasons change, night turns to day, and day to night. This has continued for thousands of years. The skies tell that we have a wonderful God who created it all. Thank you, Lord, for the beauty of creation, that tells me of your wonder and glory!

Daily Reading: Jeremiah 41-43

August 29

Revelation 7:9-10 "After this I beheld, and, lo, a great multitude, which no man could number, of all nations, and kindreds, and people, and tongues, stood before the throne, and before the Lamb, clothed with white robes, and palms in their hands; and cried with a loud voice, saying, Salvation to our God which sitteth upon the throne, and unto the Lamb."

And, lo, a great multitude...of all nations, and kindreds, and people, and tongues, stood before the throne, and before the Lamb, clothed with white robes. I have never been to a fortune teller of any kind because I know what my future is. It is written in God's Word. This Scripture talks of the saved and when we will gather together in our white robes. We will join to give worship and honor to Jesus Christ, the Lamb of God. Thank you, Lord, that I am yours, that I will join with other saints to give you praise!

_____

_____

_____

_____

Daily Reading: Jeremiah 44-46

August 30

Ephesians 1:6 "To the praise of the glory of his grace, wherein he hath made us accepted in the beloved."

Accepted in the beloved. We are accepted by Jesus, the Perfect One who had no sin. Not only does He accept us, but He is preparing a place for us in the glories of Heaven. And all because He died for us! Thank you, Lord, for accepting me, for loving me, for dying for me!

Daily Reading: Jeremiah 47-49

August 31

Ephesians 1:7 "In whom we have redemption through his blood, the forgiveness of sins, according to the riches of his grace."

We have redemption... according to the riches of his grace. Some people spend their whole life seeking riches, and when they die, they stand before God with nothing. Those who accept Jesus as Savior have accepted riches that are eternal. Those treasures are freely given to anyone who repents and trusts Christ. Thank you, Lord, that I am rich beyond measure, that you have given me your eternal treasure!

_____
_____
_____
_____
_____
_____
_____

Daily Reading: Jeremiah 50-52

September 1

Psalm 107:19 "Then they cry unto the LORD in their trouble, and he saveth them out of their distresses."

He saveth them out of their distresses. In verse 17 of this Psalm, the writer speaks of fools. We were all fools before we were saved, when we rejected the grace of God. But when we cried out to Him, He saved us. Thank you, Lord, for saving a fool like me!

Daily Reading: Lamentations 1-2

September 2

Matthew 21:43 "Therefore say I unto you, The kingdom of God shall be taken from you, and given to a nation bringing forth the fruits thereof."

The kingdom of God shall be... given to a nation bringing forth the fruits thereof. Throughout the Old Testament the Hebrew people were God's people. Even though they turned from Him time and again, He returned His blessings to them when they repented. When Christ came upon the earth, He opened the doors of Heaven to the Gentiles, that any who believed might be saved eternally. Thank you, Lord, for the gift of salvation to the Gentiles and for those who have brought the Gospel over all the world!

Daily Reading: Lamentations 3-5

September 3

Romans 8:26 "Likewise the Spirit also helpeth our infirmities: for we know not what we should pray for as we ought: but the Spirit itself maketh intercession for us with groanings which cannot be uttered."

The Spirit itself maketh intercession for us with groanings which cannot be uttered. Have you reached a point of devastation so great that you cannot speak words in prayer to God? During these times the Spirit, knowing your need and your circumstances, speaks on your behalf. Thank you, Lord, for those times, that your Holy Spirit was my spokesperson, crying to you for my comfort and deliverance!

Daily Reading: Ezekiel 1-3

September 4

Psalm 44:3 "For they got not the land in possession by their own sword, neither did their own arm save them: but thy right hand, and thine arm, and the light of thy countenance, because thou hadst a favour unto them."

For they got not the land in possession by their own sword... but thy right hand. In the Old Testament we read of wartime victories for the Israelites when they often did not even fight a battle. God's hand moved for them and destroyed their enemies. God gives us the same type of victory when we depend on Him. He does the same today. When the omnipotent God fights our enemy, our victory is never in doubt. Thank you, Lord, for entering into my battles and giving me many victories!

___

___

___

___

___

___

Daily Reading: Ezekiel 4-6

September 5

Isaiah 25:4 "For thou hast been a strength to the poor, a strength to the needy in his distress, a refuge from the storm, a shadow from the heat, when the blast of the terrible ones is as a storm against the wall."

For thou hast been a strength to the poor, a strength to the needy in his distress. God provides His strength for those who lack other resources, for the poor and needy. At times we find that we do not have a way to fight off temptations and to overcome Satan, but God gives us His power if we will call upon Him. Thank you, Lord, for your strength in times of trouble and temptation!

_____
_____
_____
_____
_____
_____

Daily Reading: Ezekiel 7-9

September 6

Isaiah 25:4 "For thou hast been a strength to the poor, a strength to the needy in his distress, a refuge from the storm, a shadow from the heat, when the blast of the terrible ones is as a storm against the wall."

For thou hast been... a refuge from the storm. In the storms of life, it is wonderful to know that you have God to call upon for His protection and care. He will come to your aid if you will just ask Him. Thank you, Lord, for the many times you have been my refuge and my sanctuary in times of trouble!

Daily Reading: Ezekiel 10-12

September 7

Isaiah 25:4 "For thou hast been a strength to the poor, a strength to the needy in his distress, a refuge from the storm, a shadow from the heat, when the blast of the terrible ones is as a storm against the wall."

For thou hast been... a shadow from the heat. In the heat of a battle, in the midst of a crisis, in a time of tribulations or trials God will shadow you. He cares for you and will cover you during trying times. Thank you, Lord, for shadowing me and providing me cover from my afflictions!

Daily Reading: Ezekiel 13-15

September 8

Isaiah 25:4 "For thou hast been a strength to the poor, a strength to the needy in his distress, a refuge from the storm, a shadow from the heat, when the blast of the terrible ones is as a storm against the wall."

For thou hast been a strength... when the blast of the terrible ones is as a storm against the wall. When you stand up for what is right and true, you sometimes find that you stand alone. When you feel like you are one battling against the world, God provides you strength. He will bless you greatly if you do not back down and when you do what is right according to His Word. Thank you, Lord, for standing with me when I war against the evils of this world!

_____
_____
_____
_____
_____
_____

Daily Reading: Ezekiel 16-18

September 9

John 15:11 "These things have I spoken unto you, that my joy might remain in you, and that your joy might be full."

These things have I spoken unto you… that your joy might be full. Jesus is speaking here to His disciples and He expresses concern with their joy. God wants Christians to be happy people, and we should be. No matter what happens to us in this short life, we have a bright and glorious future. Thank you, Lord, for the joy I experience in you!

_____
_____
_____
_____
_____
_____
_____
_____

Daily Reading: Ezekiel 19-21

September 10

Exodus 3:14 "And God said unto Moses, I AM THAT I AM: and he said, Thus shalt thou say unto the children of Israel, I AM hath sent me unto you."

And God said unto Moses, I AM THAT I AM. God spoke directly with Moses and He speaks directly to us through the written Word of God. When God stated I AM THAT I AM, He revealed to Moses that He is the self-existent One of permanent life—He is the One True God. Many false gods are in this world, but only One who always was and always will be. Thank you, Lord, for your ever-present being and for revealing yourself to me!

Daily Reading: Ezekiel 22-24

September 11

Psalm 94:18 "When I said, My foot slippeth; thy mercy, O LORD, held me up."

Thy mercy, O Lord, held me up. We sin after we are saved, but because of God's grace and mercy we are forgiven. We are held up by God's wonderful love and favor. He has promised that our sins are gone and forgotten. Thank you, Lord, for your excellent mercy and grace and for keeping me when I fall into sin!

_____
_____
_____
_____
_____
_____
_____

Daily Reading: Ezekiel 25-27

September 12

Ephesians 4:7 "But unto every one of us is given grace according to the measure of the gift of Christ."

Grace according to the measure of the gift of Christ. As children of God we are given gifts of grace: some are called to preach, some to teach, some to minister and uplift others, some to provide music or song, but all are given a measure. If we seek God's guidance, He will reveal what His plan is for each of us. Thank you, Lord, for your gifts of grace, for using me to spread the Word of your salvation!

Daily Reading: Ezekiel 28-30

September 13

Deuteronomy 28:8 "The LORD shall command the blessing upon thee in thy storehouses, and in all that thou settest thine hand unto; and he shall bless thee in the land which the LORD thy God giveth thee."

The Lord shall command the blessing upon thee in thy storehouses. One truth I have found in my life—God blesses His children abundantly. I have never been rich in material possessions according to the world's standards, but God has provided me much more than I need, and certainly more than I deserve. Thank you, Lord, for Your provision, for Your plentiful blessings!

Daily Reading: Ezekiel 31-33

September 14

1 Peter 2:22-23 *"Who did no sin, neither was guile found in his mouth: Who, when he was reviled, reviled not again; when he suffered, he threatened not; but committed himself to him that judgeth righteously."*

When he suffered, he threatened not; but committed himself to him that judgeth righteously. When Jesus Christ was crucified, He endured mocking and pain at the hands of sinful men. But He was an obedient Son, who suffered without fighting back, without reply to the peoples' scornful shouting. Thank you, Lord, for your loving example you gave me, even as you bore the suffering for my sins!

Daily Reading: Ezekiel 34-36

September 15

1 John 2:24-25 "Let that therefore abide in you, which ye have heard from the beginning. If that which ye have heard from the beginning shall remain in you, ye also shall continue in the Son, and in the Father. And this is the promise that he hath promised us, even eternal life."

And this is the promise that he hath promised us, even eternal life. Man was created with a God-breathed soul, that lives forever. If we accept the free gift of salvation and abide with God, we have an eternity with Him forever, never ending in the glories of Heaven. Thank you, Lord, for your promise of eternal life when I will dwell with You!

Daily Reading: Ezekiel 37-39

A YEAR OF THANKSGIVING

September 16

Psalm 47:2 "For the LORD most high is terrible; he is a great King over all the earth."

For the Lord most high is terrible. The Hebrew word used here, *yare'*, translated terrible, means one to be feared with great respect. Many people today have little or no fear of God and live in defiance to His Word and His commands. Satan himself is not obstinate when standing before Him. God's power and awesomeness are evident. We will all be humbled before Him. Thank you, Lord, that you are all powerful and all knowing. You alone are God!

Daily Reading: Ezekiel 40-42

September 17

Hebrews 11:3 "Through faith we understand that the worlds were framed by the word of God, so that things which are seen were not made of things which do appear."

Things which are seen were not made of things which do appear. God's creation is awesome, created by just the Word of His mouth. Advancing technology reveals even more the wonder of what God has created. Men have studied and researched the universe for many years, but much is still not understood by man's limited intelligence. Thank you, Lord, for the wonders of our world and for revealing to me that I am a precious part of your creation!

Daily Reading: Ezekiel 43-45

September 18

Titus 2:13 "Looking for that blessed hope, and the glorious appearing of the great God and our Saviour Jesus Christ."

Looking for that blessed hope... Jesus Christ. As I write this amid the pandemic of 2020, the world is in a major state of panic. Those of us who are Christians know that events like these are foretold in God's Word, and we know from His Word that He is in control and our hope is in Jesus. Humans are weak and vulnerable, and hopeless without Jesus as their God. Thank you, Lord, for the hope You have revealed to me in your blessed Word!

_____

_____

_____

_____

_____

_____

Daily Reading: Ezekiel 46-48

September 19

Titus 2:14 "Who gave himself for us, that he might redeem us from all iniquity, and purify unto himself a peculiar people, zealous of good works."

Who gave himself for us, that he might redeem us from all iniquity. Jesus suffered a cruel death on the cross that any person who trusts and believes that He is God and Savior will be saved. Jesus arose from the grave on the third day, victorious over death. He gives His children the same victory, that we may spend eternity with Him in Heaven. Thank you, Lord, for your death and resurrection, for in that is my hope!

Daily Reading: Daniel 1-3

September 20

Psalm 12:6-7 "The words of the LORD are pure words: as silver tried in a furnace of earth, purified seven times. Thou shalt keep them, O LORD, thou shalt preserve them from this generation for ever."

The words of the Lord are pure words... thou shalt keep them. The Word of God is tried and true and will be preserved forever. It is impossible for God to lie (Titus 1:2). His Word was written by men who were given the Scriptures by the breath of the Holy Spirit. We can trust God and we can trust His Word to be holy and true. Thank you, Lord, for your Word, the Bible, for by it I have received eternal life in you!

Daily Reading: Daniel 4-6

September 21

Revelation 7:17 "For the Lamb which is in the midst of the throne shall feed them, and shall lead them unto living fountains of waters: and God shall wipe away all tears from their eyes."

And God shall wipe away all tears from their eyes. The time is coming when there will be no more sorrow and no parting and all will be joy. This is a promise to those who love God and who have trusted Jesus as their Savior. In contrast, those who fail to believe will be banished to the pits of hell, to an eternity of weeping and gnashing of teeth. Thank you, Lord, for the time coming when I no longer will shed tears, but all will be joy and happiness!

Daily Reading: Daniel 7-9

September 22

Ephesians 1:15-16 "Wherefore I also, after I heard of your faith in the Lord Jesus, and love unto all the saints, cease not to give thanks for you, making mention of you in my prayers."

Give thanks for you, making mention of you in my prayers. In Paul's letter to the Ephesians he tells them that he thanks God for them and that he prays for them. What a blessing to know that someone is praying for you! We all need prayer, as we all need the power of God upon us. Thank you, Lord, for the prayers of those who love me and pray for me!

Daily Reading: Daniel 10-12

September 23

2 Corinthians 12:9 "And he said unto me, My grace is sufficient for thee: for my strength is made perfect in weakness. Most gladly therefore will I rather glory in my infirmities, that the power of Christ may rest upon me."

My strength is made perfect in weakness. We all are just one heartbeat from dying a physical death. During serious illness, we are made to realize our weakness, and it is then that many turn to the Lord for strength. God is omnipotent, the One with power to overcome sickness, sin, and death. Thank you, Lord, for your power and might, that gives me the ability to overcome what I could never defeat without you!

_____
_____
_____
_____
_____
_____
_____

Daily Reading: Hosea 1-4

September 24

Psalm 117:1-2 "O praise the LORD, all ye nations: praise him, all ye people. For his merciful kindness is great toward us: and the truth of the LORD endureth for ever. Praise ye the LORD."

His merciful kindness is great toward us. God has been so good to us, extending mercy to undeserving sinners. Left in our lost state, we were headed for the pits of hell. He sought us, like lost sheep, and brought us to His care and protection when He saved our souls. Thank you, Lord, for your grace and mercy that saved me, a wicked sinner!

_____
_____
_____
_____
_____
_____
_____

Daily Reading: Hosea 5-8

September 25

Romans 9:26 "And it shall come to pass, that in the place where it was said unto them, Ye are not my people; there shall they be called the children of the living God."

There shall they be called the children of the living God. The Jewish people of the Old Testament were God's Chosen People. The prophet Hosea foretold that a people not of the Hebrew nation would be called the children of the living God, speaking of Gentiles (Hosea 2:23). Since Jesus came to this earth, salvation is offered to any who will repent and believe that He is the Son of God. Thank you, Lord, for extending salvation to me, a Gentile, an unworthy sinner!

_____
_____
_____
_____
_____
_____
_____

Daily Reading: Hosea 9-11

September 26

Psalm 44:7 "But thou hast saved us from our enemies, and hast put them to shame that hated us."

Thou hast saved us from our enemies. If you generally get along with most people, you may think you have no enemies. As a Christian you have adversaries. They might be people whom you think are friends. The demons of darkness are enemies who want to harm you and your Christian testimony. God will save you from the opposition if you remain close to your Lord and Defender. Thank you, Lord, for protecting me from Satan's darts as he tries to lead me away from you!

_____

_____

_____

_____

_____

_____

_____

Daily Reading: Hosea 12-14

September 27

Psalm 127:3 "Lo, children are an heritage of the LORD: and the fruit of the womb is his reward."

Children are an heritage of the Lord. The beauty and innocence of a small child is a blessing. Little children bring joy to households, and to those around them. Even though born with a sinful nature, a baby can remind us of the purity, simplicity and trustfulness of Adam and Eve before they fell into sin. They had a wonderful relationship with God. Our relationship should be similar, when we totally trust Jesus with our lives and obey His Word. Thank you, Lord, for the loveliness and innocence of little babies. Help me to be as one of them—relying and trusting fully in you!

Daily Reading: Joel 1-3

September 28

Ecclesiastes 7:2 "It is better to go to the house of mourning, than to go to the house of feasting: for that is the end of all men; and the living will lay it to his heart."

It is better to go to the house of mourning... for that is the end of all men; and the living will lay it to his heart. All will die and stand before God in judgment. It is better that people mourn death than to feast and celebrate because seeing the dead reminds us that we all will die one day. Death is no respecter of persons or age—it may come to anyone at any time. Therefore, we must be ready, saved and living for Jesus. Do not delay, for tomorrow is promised to no one. Thank you, Lord, for the reminder that my time on this earth is short. Let me live every moment for your glory and honor!

Daily Reading: Amos 1-3

September 29

John 17:6 "I have manifested thy name unto the men which thou gavest me out of the world: thine they were, and thou gavest them me; and they have kept thy word."

Thou gavest them me; and they have kept thy word. Jesus chose apostles and disciples to follow Him while He was on this earth, and after His death, to spread the Word of God to the world. Certain of these men wrote the books of the New Testament as guided by the Holy Spirit. Thank you, Lord, for these men who kept your Word and for those who later brought your Word to me, that I might be saved!

_____
_____
_____
_____
_____
_____
_____

Daily Reading: Amos 4-6

September 30

Psalm 113:7-8 "He raiseth up the poor out of the dust, and lifteth the needy out of the dunghill; that he may set him with princes, even with the princes of his people."

He raiseth up the poor out of the dust. Jesus told His disciples that it was easier for a rich man to go through the eye of a needle than to enter the kingdom of God. He was telling them that the rich often make their wealth their god and do not seek after the Savior. The poor see their need and trust Jesus and are given riches that far surpass the value of the fortunes of this world. Thank you, Lord, for the abundance you have given me in Jesus, for my inheritance is treasure untold!

Daily Reading: Amos 7-9, Obadiah 1

October 1

Isaiah 64:8 "But now, O LORD, thou art our father; we are the clay, and thou our potter; and we all are the work of thy hand."

We are the clay, and thou our potter; and we all are the work of thy hand. God shapes us to make us beautiful vessels to bring Him honor and glory. We are the clay. It is amazing to see the beauty created with a lump of clay that He shapes and molds with His will. Thank you, Lord, for repairing my flaws, for shaping me to be a vessel of honor for you!

Daily Reading: Jonah 1-4

October 2

Psalm 118:24 "This is the day which the LORD hath made; we will rejoice and be glad in it."

This is the day which the Lord hath made. God blesses us with each day, twenty-four hours to give Him thanksgiving and praise. We have opportunities each day to tell others of God's saving grace, to pray, to read His Word, and to do the work He has guided us to do. Thank you, Lord, for each day you have given me—let me use each waking hour for your honor!

Daily Reading: Micah 1-4

October 3

Psalm 33:12 "Blessed is the nation whose God is the LORD; and the people whom he hath chosen for his own inheritance."

Blessed is the nation whose God is the Lord. From the time that the Europeans came to settle in the United States, God has blessed this nation. We live in a nation of abundant resources, plentiful land, and from coast to coast, a beautiful creation of God. As the populace becomes more sinful and turns from God's will, He withholds His blessings upon us. We must turn back to Him. Thank you, Lord, for putting me in this nation, exceedingly favored by your hand!

Daily Reading: Micah 5-7

October 4

Romans 5:3 "And not only so, but we glory in tribulations also: knowing that tribulation worketh patience."

Tribulation worketh patience. Are there trials and tribulations in your life? Thank the Lord for these, for they strengthen your patience. Like an anvil, we are made strong with afflictions and sorrows. Trials make us more empathetic to the misfortune and misery of others. Thank you, Lord, for the tribulations, grief, and hardships you have allowed me to experience, for in them, I have drawn closer to you!

_____
_____
_____
_____
_____
_____
_____

Daily Reading: Nahum 1-3

October 5

Psalm 103:17 "But the mercy of the LORD is from everlasting to everlasting upon them that fear him, and his righteousness unto children's children."

The mercy of the Lord is from everlasting to everlasting. The word "mercy" means compassionate treatment, not receiving what is deserved. Because of our sin, we deserve an eternity in hell, but by God's mercy we are saved from damnation by faith through grace. What a merciful God is He! Thank you, Lord, for your mercy upon me, that I may have the hope of eternity in Heaven!

_____
_____
_____
_____
_____
_____
_____

Daily Reading: Habakkuk 1-3

October 6

2 Corinthians 4:8-9 *"We are troubled on every side, yet not distressed; we are perplexed, but not in despair; persecuted, but not forsaken; cast down, but not destroyed."*

We are troubled on every side, yet not distressed. In this world you have troubles that at times are overwhelming. Go to Jesus. He will take your burdens upon Himself and give you relief and rest. Thank you, Lord, for your care, for lightening my load, for giving me deliverance!

Daily Reading: Zephaniah 1-3

October 7

2 Corinthians 4:8-9 *"We are troubled on every side, yet not distressed; we are perplexed, but not in despair; persecuted, but not forsaken; cast down, but not destroyed."*

We are perplexed, but not in despair. Are you unsure what to do, what direction to take in your life? Do not despair, take it to Jesus. He will direct you in the way you should go, giving you assurance when you follow Him. Thank you, Lord, for your guiding hand in my life—you have never steered me wrong!

Daily Reading: Haggai 1-2, Zechariah 1-2

October 8

2 Corinthians 4:8-9 "We are troubled on every side, yet not distressed; we are perplexed, but not in despair; persecuted, but not forsaken; cast down, but not destroyed."

Persecuted, but not forsaken. We often face persecution for our Christian faith. The world thinks we are peculiar, that our faith is weakness. Our Lord is our strength. Yes, we are different from the world, for we are children of the Most High God. Thank you, Lord, that you are with me through any oppression or discrimination, for you have never forsaken me!

Daily Reading: Zechariah 3-5

October 9

2 Corinthians 4:8-9 "We are troubled on every side, yet not distressed; we are perplexed, but not in despair; persecuted, but not forsaken; cast down, but not destroyed."

Cast down, but not destroyed. Christians have been cast down: treated badly by teachers, discriminated in employment, and shunned by friends and family because of our faith in God. However, we are not destroyed. We are strengthened by these actions. We are honored to be persecuted for the cause of Christ. Thank you, Lord, for lifting me up, for giving me the strength to stand for you!

Daily Reading: Zechariah 6-8

October 10

Jude 1:2 "Mercy unto you, and peace, and love, be multiplied."

Peace, and love, be multiplied. Are you resting in the arms of Jesus? Are you trusting in His love? What a wonderful feeling of peace and comfort are provided when you live in God's will. You have the knowledge of His protection and His mercy, and nothing can harm you. Thank you, Lord, for your blessed hand upon me, that you loved me enough to die for my sins!

Daily Reading: Zechariah 9-11

October 11

Esther 4:14 "For if thou altogether holdest thy peace at this time, then shall there enlargement and deliverance arise to the Jews from another place; but thou and thy father's house shall be destroyed: and who knoweth whether thou art come to the kingdom for such a time as this?"

Who knoweth whether thou art come to the kingdom for such a time as this? Life takes unexpected turns, and we often wonder why things occur the way they do. God has a plan. As we age, we look back over the past and we can see how God orchestrated things in our lives so that His will is carried out according to His plan. Thank you, Lord, for working in my life, for taking control and for placing me where you want me!

_____
_____
_____
_____
_____
_____
_____

Daily Reading: Zechariah 12-14

October 12

1 Thessalonians 2:9 "For ye remember, brethren, our labour and travail: for labouring night and day, because we would not be chargeable unto any of you, we preached unto you the gospel of God."

We preached unto you the gospel of God. Paul reminded the Christians at Thessalonica of the work that he and Silvanus and Timothy did when they were there, and he encouraged them in their labors for the Lord. A preacher of the Word must be an example to those he leads, teaching and obeying God's Word, and in being a fellow worker performing tasks that need to be done. Thank you, Lord, for the preachers and pastors I have known who expounded your Word, giving me a better knowledge of you!

_____
_____
_____
_____
_____
_____

Daily Reading: Malachi 1-4

October 13

Titus 3:5 "Not by works of righteousness which we have done, but according to his mercy he saved us, by the washing of regeneration, and renewing of the Holy Ghost."

Not by works of righteousness which we have done, but according to his mercy. Because of our sin, no amount of good works can save us, only the blood of Jesus. His blood is our righteousness. Without God's mercy, love, and goodness we would be bound for hell. Thank you, Lord, for saving me by your grace and mercy, for in me is no virtue without Jesus!

Daily Reading: Matthew 1-4

October 14

Psalm 68:6 "God setteth the solitary in families: he bringeth out those which are bound with chains: but the rebellious dwell in a dry land."

God setteth the solitary in families. A wonderful fellowship is found within Christian churches. For the lonely, there is family: brothers and sisters in Christ. We share our sadness, troubles, and heartaches, and our joys and celebrations with our fellow Christians. Thank you, Lord, for my Christian brothers and sisters and for the close communion I have with them!

_____
_____
_____
_____
_____
_____
_____

Daily Reading: Matthew 5-7

October 15

Psalm 68:6 "God setteth the solitary in families: he bringeth out those which are bound with chains: but the rebellious dwell in a dry land."

He bringeth out those which are bound with chains. Before we were saved, we were bound by the chains of sin. Some were bound with addictions, some with fleshly desires, some with pride, etc., but we all were slaves to sin in our lives. When we trust Jesus as Savior, He gives us the power to overcome the sin that binds us. Thank you, Lord, for the freedom you have given me, free from those chains which held me!

Daily Reading: Matthew 8-10

October 16

1 Peter 4:13 "But rejoice, inasmuch as ye are partakers of Christ's sufferings; that, when his glory shall be revealed, ye may be glad also with exceeding joy."

Rejoice, inasmuch as ye are partakers of Christ's sufferings. Have you suffered for the cause of Christ? If so, rejoice. That may be difficult to do in this life, but this verse tells that we will be exceedingly joyful when Jesus' glory is revealed to us. A greater blessing will be ours when we stand before God and the glory will be to Jesus, our King. Thank you, Lord, for all the hardships and afflictions I have endured for you, for they will be to your honor in the end!

Daily Reading: Matthew 11-13

October 17

Hebrews 13:5 "Let your conversation be without covetousness; and be content with such things as ye have: for he hath said, I will never leave thee, nor forsake thee."

For he hath said, I will never leave thee, nor forsake thee. In whatever situation we may find ourselves we can hold to this promise, that God will never forsake us. He is with us during the good times as well as during the dark hours of grieving, heartache, sickness, and tribulations. Thank you, Lord, for ever being with me, even during the times that my faith is failing!

Daily Reading: Matthew 14-16

October 18

Joshua 1:8 "This book of the law shall not depart out of thy mouth; but thou shalt meditate therein day and night, that thou mayest observe to do according to all that is written therein: for then thou shalt make thy way prosperous, and then thou shalt have good success."

Thou shalt meditate therein day and night, that thou mayest observe to do according to all that is written therein. How can we obey God if we do not know what He requires of us? We have a responsibility to read and know God's Word that we may obey its precepts. Thank you, Lord, for preserving your Word, that I may bring you honor and glory with my obedience!

_____
_____
_____
_____
_____
_____

Daily Reading: Matthew 17-19

October 19

Colossians 1:21 "And you, that were sometime alienated and enemies in your mind by wicked works, yet now hath he reconciled."

And you, that were sometime alienated and enemies… yet now hath he reconciled. If you have rejected God's gift of salvation and continue to live life without Jesus, you are an enemy of God. That is a frightening situation. God is powerful and just, and all will stand before Him in judgment one day. But you may be reconciled and saved by trusting and believing Jesus. Thank you, Lord, for drawing me away from my sinful life, for saving me and making me yours!

Daily Reading: Matthew 20-22

October 20

Psalm 74:16-17 "The day is thine, the night also is thine: thou hast prepared the light and the sun. Thou hast set all the borders of the earth: thou hast made summer and winter."

Thou hast prepared the light and the sun... thou hast made summer and winter. Over thousands of years, the earth has continued to rotate around the sun. Seasons have remained constant year after year: winter to spring, spring to summer, summer to fall, and fall to winter. God controls the light and the sun and the seasons. Thank you, Lord, for the beauty of nature and for your control over the seasons and over all creation!

_____
_____
_____
_____
_____
_____
_____

Daily Reading: Matthew 23-25

October 21

Revelation 21:27 "And there shall in no wise enter into it any thing that defileth, neither whatsoever worketh abomination, or maketh a lie: but they which are written in the Lamb's book of life."

There shall in no wise enter into it any thing... but they which are written in the Lamb's book of life. This chapter of Revelation speaks of the New Jerusalem, where the saved will dwell forever with Jesus. Before we were saved, in God's all-knowing power, our names were written in the Lamb's Book of Life. Only those whose names are written there will be in Heaven. Nothing that defiles, that is stained with sin, may enter. The sin of the saved has been washed clean by the blood of Jesus. Thank you, Lord, that you have saved me, that my name is written there, and that I will dwell with Jesus!

Daily Reading: Matthew 26-28

October 22

Psalm 116:1-2 "I love the LORD, because he hath heard my voice and my supplications. Because he hath inclined his ear unto me, therefore will I call upon him as long as I live."

I love the Lord, because he hath heard my voice and my supplications. When we call to Him in faith, God hears our voice. The God who created all the universe, who is all-powerful, all-knowing hears our voice! Scripture tells us again and again that God cares for us, that He hears our cry. Thank you, Lord, for hearing my prayers and my praise!

_____

_____

_____

_____

_____

_____

_____

Daily Reading: Mark 1-4

October 23

Acts 22:28 "And the chief captain answered, With a great sum obtained I this freedom. And Paul said, But I was free born."

With a great sum obtained I this freedom… but I was free born. Even though this is a conversation between Paul and a chief captain, these words can be applied to our lives. With a great sum, or price, I obtained this freedom—Christ died on the cross, the price for our salvation; but I was free born—salvation, our new birth, was provided a free gift to us. Thank you, Lord, for Jesus, who paid the great price with His life, and who set me free!

_____
_____
_____
_____
_____
_____
_____
_____

Daily Reading: Mark 5-7

October 24

Psalm 31:19 "Oh how great is thy goodness, which thou hast laid up for them that fear thee; which thou hast wrought for them that trust in thee before the sons of men!"

Oh how great is thy goodness. Dwell just a while on the goodness of God, of all the many blessings He has given us. We could not begin to count all His kindnesses. Give Him all your praises and worship for all the many wonderful things He has done for us. Thank you, Lord, for your righteousness, your virtue, and your honor, for you have been so good to me!

_____

_____

_____

_____

_____

_____

_____

Daily Reading: Mark 8-10

October 25

Exodus 14:13 "And Moses said unto the people, Fear ye not, stand still, and see the salvation of the LORD, which he will shew to you to day: for the Egyptians whom ye have seen to day, ye shall see them again no more for ever."

Fear ye not, stand still, and see the salvation of the Lord. What kind of evil is chasing after you? Is it temptation, worry, fear? You are told to stand still. Stop trying to solve your problems in your own power and look to God for His strength. He will destroy your enemies and you will see them no more! Thank you, Lord, for eliminating the adversaries in my life, for overcoming with your power!

Daily Reading: Mark 11-13

October 26

Hebrews 2:6-7 "But one in a certain place testified, saying, What is man, that thou art mindful of him? or the son of man, that thou visitest him? Thou madest him a little lower than the angels; thou crownedst him with glory and honour, and didst set him over the works of thy hands."

What is man? Thou... didst set him over the works of thy hands. God placed man upon this earth and put him over all creation. We have an intelligence far superior to any other living organism. This is a great privilege. With great privilege comes great responsibility. Man must care for the earth and God's creation. Failure to do so will bring God's judgment. Thank you, Lord, for giving me intelligence and dominion, help me to use it wisely for your honor and glory!

Daily Reading: Mark 14-16

October 27

Psalm 128:1-2 "Blessed is every one that feareth the LORD; that walketh in his ways. For thou shalt eat the labour of thine hands: happy shalt thou be, and it shall be well with thee."

Blessed is every one that feareth the Lord... it shall be well with thee. When we are saved and walking with the Lord, we are greatly favored by God. As a child who experiences undying love from his Father, we have joy, happiness, and many blessings from God's hand. Thank you, Lord, for your love and care for me, your precious child!

_____
_____
_____
_____
_____
_____
_____

Daily Reading: Luke 1-3

October 28

Isaiah 9:6 "For unto us a child is born, unto us a son is given: and the government shall be upon his shoulder: and his name shall be called Wonderful, Counsellor, The mighty God, The everlasting Father, The Prince of Peace."

For unto us a child is born… and the government shall be upon his shoulder. The time is coming that Jesus will be the only government head for all the world. We will see the end of lying and corrupt government leaders, and the end of battles and wars. It will be a time of perfect peace and harmony. Thank you, Lord, that I may look forward to that time, when you will be the only Ruler, Prince, and King!

_____
_____
_____
_____
_____
_____

Daily Reading: Luke 4-6

October 29

Colossians 2:4-5 "And this I say, lest any man should beguile you with enticing words. For though I be absent in the flesh, yet am I with you in the spirit, joying and beholding your order, and the stedfastness of your faith in Christ."

Though I be absent in the flesh, yet am I with you in the spirit. In Paul's letter to the Colossians, he stated he was confident that the Christians there were following God's will. We cannot always be with our children, but if they have been taught well from God's Word, we can have the same confidence. Thank you, Lord, for guiding me as a parent, and for guiding my children to do your will!

Daily Reading: Luke 7-9

October 30

2 Timothy 2:1-2 "Thou therefore, my son, be strong in the grace that is in Christ Jesus. And the things that thou hast heard of me among many witnesses, the same commit thou to faithful men, who shall be able to teach others also."

The things that thou hast heard of me… the same commit thou to faithful men, who shall be able to teach others also. God uses faithful men to teach and preach the Word of God, and He uses elder, wiser men to guide the younger ones. Paul told Timothy that as he learned from his example, Timothy was to teach other faithful men. Thank you, Lord, for those aged and enlightened individuals who you placed in my life, who taught me many good things of you!

_____
_____
_____
_____
_____
_____

Daily Reading: Luke 10-12

October 31

Psalm 12:6 "The words of the LORD are pure words: as silver tried in a furnace of earth, purified seven times."

The words of the Lord are pure words. Many treasures are found in the reading of God's Word—Words of wisdom, of beauty, of grace, of salvation. And the fire within those Words burns at your heart like no other writings! Thank you, Lord, for giving me your Word, for I love to read the Holy Bible!

_____

_____

_____

_____

_____

_____

Daily Reading: Luke 13-15

November 1

Revelation 3:12 "Him that overcometh will I make a pillar in the temple of my God, and he shall go no more out: and I will write upon him the name of my God, and the name of the city of my God, which is new Jerusalem, which cometh down out of heaven from my God: and I will write upon him my new name."

I will write upon him my new name. When a woman marries, traditionally she is given the surname of her husband, showing commitment and love, oneness, and unity. When we are taken into Heaven, we, the bride of Christ, are given a new name, His name. What better name to have than the name of Jesus! I look forward to that day like a bride anticipates her wedding day. Thank you, Lord, that I will be named for you, that I will be a part of your bride!

___
___
___
___
___

Daily Reading: Luke 16-18

November 2

Psalm 86:5 "For thou, Lord, art good, and ready to forgive; and plenteous in mercy unto all them that call upon thee."

For thou, Lord, art good, and ready to forgive. Have you sinned today? Do not despair. As the psalmist said, God is good, and He is ready to forgive you. No need for guilt, no need for worry. Repent and pray for forgiveness and He will grant it! Thank you, Lord, for your wonderful goodness, that my sins are forgiven and forgotten!

Daily Reading: Luke 19-21

November 3

2 Peter 1:10 "Wherefore the rather, brethren, give diligence to make your calling and election sure: for if ye do these things, ye shall never fall."

Make your calling and election sure: for if ye do these things, ye shall never fall. Some believe that a person may be saved and later lose salvation because of sin, but Scripture tells us differently. You are told to be sure of your calling and election. Examine your heart—have you really had a changed life? Do you truly love Jesus? Is He God of all in your life? If you can answer yes, then glory to God, you are saved! Thank you, Lord, for giving me the gift of salvation, that I am forever in your hand!

_____

_____

_____

_____

_____

_____

Daily Reading: Luke 22-24

November 4

James 5:7 "Be patient therefore, brethren, unto the coming of the Lord. Behold, the husbandman waiteth for the precious fruit of the earth, and hath long patience for it, until he receive the early and latter rain."

The husbandman waiteth for the precious fruit... and hath long patience for it. As a farmer patiently waits for the crops to appear and ripen, Christians are to await the marvelous time when Christ will return to call His saints home. Farmers in the Middle Eastern areas wait for two rainy seasons that will occur before the harvest time is right, as we must await the day God has appointed for us. Thank you, Lord, that I will be among your saints, called away on that wonderful, glorious day!

Daily Reading: John 1-3

November 5

2 Chronicles 14:11a "And Asa cried unto the LORD his God, and said, LORD, it is nothing with thee to help, whether with many, or with them that have no power: help us, O LORD our God."

It is nothing with thee to help. The God who spoke the Word and put the earth and all creation into existence is an all-powerful God. Asa realized this, and when he petitioned God for help, reminded God that doing this is nothing to Him, it was an easy task for the Lord to overcome Asa's enemies. Thank you, Lord, for your might and strength, that you can defeat my enemies with your power!

_____

_____

_____

_____

_____

_____

_____

Daily Reading: John 4-6

November 6

1 Corinthians 15:10a "But by the grace of God I am what I am: and his grace which was bestowed upon me was not in vain."

By the grace of God I am what I am. Have you ever considered what kind of life you may have led if you had not been saved? Salvation not only changes your heart but also your path in life. Unless you were saved at an early age, most likely you were headed in the wrong direction when Jesus turned you around and saved your soul. Thank you, Lord, for making a change in me, and for making my life one that is for your glory!

Daily Reading: John 7-9

November 7

1 Corinthians 15:10b "But I laboured more abundantly than they all: yet not I, but the grace of God which was with me."

But I laboured more abundantly than they all. If you are employed, do you work harder than your co-workers? Do you give more effort and conduct yourself above reproach? If so, do not pat yourself on the back, but give God the thanks, because as this verse states, it was God's grace. Thank you, Lord, for putting in me the will to please you, at my place of work, in my church and in my home!

Daily Reading: John 10-12

November 8

Psalm 115:11 "Ye that fear the LORD, trust in the LORD: he is their help and their shield."

He is their help and their shield. You may not see the need in today's world for a shield, but Satan is aiming his fiery darts at you, trying to tempt you and draw you away from God and His protective hand. God is your help. He has the power to defeat your enemy and to keep you safe. Thank you, Lord, for your help and protection in all the battles of my life!

_____
_____
_____
_____
_____
_____
_____
_____

Daily Reading: John 13-15

November 9

Romans 1:16 "For I am not ashamed of the gospel of Christ: for it is the power of God unto salvation to every one that believeth; to the Jew first, and also to the Greek."

It is the power of God unto salvation to every one that believeth. The Gospel, the Living Word, burns in our hearts and has the power to change lives. The word dynamite originated from the Greek word for power used in this phrase: Words so powerful they can take us all the way to Heaven. And these Words can bring salvation to anyone who will believe, Jew or Gentile. Thank you, Lord, that the power of your Words exploded a change in my heart and my life!

___
___
___
___
___
___
___

Daily Reading: John 16-18

November 10

Psalm 33:16 "There is no king saved by the multitude of an host: a mighty man is not delivered by much strength."

A mighty man is not delivered by much strength. A person is often shown by God to lack strength or ability, even though they may be strong, healthy, and intelligent. God wants His people to look to Him, to depend upon Him for success and victory, and God wants the glory for those victories. Thank you, Lord, for humbling me when I did not depend on you and failed in my own abilities. Thank you for showing me that you are my power and my strength, and the source of my success and victory!

_____

_____

_____

_____

_____

_____

Daily Reading: John 19-21

November 11

Exodus 15:6 "Thy right hand, O LORD, is become glorious in power: thy right hand, O LORD, hath dashed in pieces the enemy."

Thy right hand, O Lord, hath dashed in pieces the enemy. God parted the Red Sea so that Moses could lead the Israelites across. After all were safely on the other side, God let the waters return, destroying Pharaoh's armies who were pursuing them. Moses then sang this song of praise and worship to God for His great power in saving His people. Thank you, Lord, for destroying my enemies, for saving me from those who pursue me to do great harm!

Daily Reading: Acts 1-3

November 12

Galatians 2:20 "I am crucified with Christ: nevertheless I live; yet not I, but Christ liveth in me: and the life which I now live in the flesh I live by the faith of the Son of God, who loved me, and gave himself for me."

The life which I now live in the flesh I live by the faith of the Son of God. A Christian's life should change dramatically after being saved. Thoughts and actions should be guided by the Lord, with a goal to please Him in everything. Are you saved? Does your life show others that you are saved? Thank you, Lord, that I have a changed life, that you live in me!

Daily Reading: Acts 4-7

November 13

Revelation 21:25 "And the gates of it shall not be shut at all by day: for there shall be no night there."

There shall be no night there. As night comes, most people lock their doors and secure their homes. Here in Revelation, God gives John a glimpse of Heaven, where the gates are always open, with no need to close them. Heaven, where Jesus is the light, and where there is no night. Thank you, Lord, for that peek into the glories of Heaven. I look forward to the day when I will enter in!

_____

_____

_____

_____

_____

_____

Daily Reading: Acts 8-10

November 14

Psalm 40:5a "Many, O LORD my God, are thy wonderful works which thou hast done, and thy thoughts which are to us-ward."

Many, O Lord my God, are... thy thoughts which are to us-ward. This meditation blesses our souls: that God, the Maker of all, thinks of us—lowly sinners who often reject Him and His Word. Not only does He think of us, He sent His Son, Jesus, to die for us. Thank you, Lord, that you remember me, care for me, and that you sent Jesus to save me!

_____
_____
_____
_____
_____
_____
_____

Daily Reading: Acts 11-13

November 15

Romans 8:16-17a "The Spirit itself beareth witness with our spirit, that we are the children of God: and if children, then heirs; heirs of God, and joint-heirs with Christ."

We are the children of God: and if children, then heirs; heirs of God, and joint-heirs with Christ. The most common source of inheritance is from parents to child, but at times, this relationship becomes strained or broken, and the child is "written out of the will". As children of God, at times our relationship is broken because of sin, but once our names are written into the Lamb's book of life, we are assured of our endowment from God. He will never write us out. Thank you, Lord, for making me your child, and for the future estate you have promised me in your Word!

Daily Reading: Acts 14-16

November 16

Psalm 100:5 "For the LORD is good; his mercy is everlasting; and his truth endureth to all generations."

The Lord is good; his mercy is everlasting. Concentrate on God's goodness today. Look at all that He has provided us: a beautiful world of nature, loving families, and He has abundantly provided well above our needs for survival. Best of all, He has given His Son, that through His grace and mercy we might be saved and will be given a home eternally in Heaven. Yes, the Lord is GOOD!! Thank you, Lord, for your goodness and mercy on me, an undeserving sinner!

Daily Reading: Acts 17-19

November 17

Hebrews 9:28 "So Christ was once offered to bear the sins of many; and unto them that look for him shall he appear the second time without sin unto salvation."

Christ was once offered to bear the sins of many; and unto them that look for him shall he appear the second time. Two certainties of life are that our human bodies will die, and we will go before God in judgment. Jesus bore the sins of those who believe and trust in Him, and when He returns He delivers us from the punishment of our wrongdoing; we will appear before God, sinless and perfect in Jesus. Thank you, Lord, for cleansing me from sin, for saving me from God's judgment!

Daily Reading: Acts 20-22

November 18

Isaiah 60:5 "Then thou shalt see, and flow together, and thine heart shall fear, and be enlarged; because the abundance of the sea shall be converted unto thee, the forces of the Gentiles shall come unto thee."

Thine heart shall fear, and be enlarged; because the abundance of the sea shall be converted unto thee. It is a joyful day when a loved one accepts Jesus as Savior. This speaks of hearts swelling with joy at the conversion of many Gentiles unto the Lord. The Bible tells us that even the angels rejoice when a sinner repents and is saved (Luke 15:10). Thank you, Lord, for my salvation, that you brought me to the knowledge of my need for you!

Daily Reading: Acts 23-25

November 19

Exodus 15:18 "The LORD shall reign for ever and ever."

The Lord shall reign for ever. One day, Jesus will call His saints home and He will reign in Heaven, surrounded by those saved by His shed blood. We will worship and glorify Him for all eternity, casting our crowns at His feet, for He is worthy of all praise. Thank you, Lord, for the future I have with you as my King!

_____

_____

_____

_____

_____

_____

_____

_____

Daily Reading: Acts 26-28

November 20

Psalm 118:18 "The LORD hath chastened me sore: but he hath not given me over unto death."

The Lord hath chastened me… but he hath not given me over unto death. When we sin after salvation, God punishes us, sometimes for the remainder of our lives. But He never takes away the grace of our salvation because Jesus suffered death for all our sins. Thank you, Lord, for the assurance that I will never suffer eternal death, because Jesus died for me!

Daily Reading: Romans 1-3

November 21

Ephesians 2:8 "For by grace are ye saved through faith; and that not of yourselves: it is the gift of God."

For by grace are ye saved through faith… it is the gift of God. Grace is defined as unmerited favor, given but not earned in any way. As this verse says, salvation is a gift freely given. Without God's grace we would all be doomed to the fires of hell. Thank you, Lord, for your grace given to me, that I may come before you in judgment, cleansed from all sin!

_____

_____

_____

_____

_____

_____

_____

_____

Daily Reading: Romans 4-7

November 22

James 5:20 "Let him know, that he which converteth the sinner from the error of his way shall save a soul from death, and shall hide a multitude of sins."

He which converteth the sinner from the error of his way shall save a soul from death. Do you have concern for lost souls? You come face to face with them every day: at the grocery, at the bank, nearly every place you go. When you share God's Word with others, when you are pleasant in your dealings with people, you may help to guide them to the Lord. Thank you, Lord, for putting people in my paths of life on whom I may have had a positive influence, who may seek you because of something I have done or said!

_____

_____

_____

_____

_____

_____

_____

Daily Reading: Romans 8-10

November 23

1 John 3:22 "And whatsoever we ask, we receive of him, because we keep his commandments, and do those things that are pleasing in his sight."

And whatsoever we ask, we receive of him, because we keep his commandments. A condition to God answering our prayers is that we live in His will and obey His commandments. Before bringing petitions before the Lord, ask Him to reveal your sin to you and ask forgiveness of all your sin. Then bring your prayers to God, with faith that He will grant your petitions. Thank you, Lord, for the many prayers you have answered, and for forgiving me when I fail to please you!

Daily Reading: Romans 11-13

November 24

Psalm 94:16-17 "Who will rise up for me against the evildoers? or who will stand up for me against the workers of iniquity? Unless the LORD had been my help, my soul had almost dwelt in silence."

Unless the Lord had been my help, my soul had almost dwelt in silence. Who will stand with you for good, battling against sin and evil? Rarely will you get a volunteer. But when you stand up for the will of God and for righteousness, the Lord will be your help. He will encourage you and give you the victory. Thank you, Lord, for giving me the strength and courage to battle against sin and wickedness in this world!

Daily Reading: Romans 14-16

A YEAR OF THANKSGIVING

November 25

1 John 4:12 "No man hath seen God at any time. If we love one another, God dwelleth in us, and his love is perfected in us."

If we love one another, God dwelleth in us. How can we say we love God if we fail to love our brothers and sisters in Christ? At times, a person will hold grudges against another, never forgiving someone for doing them wrong. This verse says that God's love is perfected IN US when we love one another! Thank you, Lord, for the love other Christians have shown to me, and I pray that I will always show your love to others!

_____
_____
_____
_____
_____
_____
_____

Daily Reading: 1 Corinthians 1-3

November 26

Job 19:25 "For I know that my redeemer liveth, and that he shall stand at the latter day upon the earth."

For I know that my redeemer liveth. In several ways we can know that Jesus lives: God's Word tells us that He lives and sits at the Father's right hand; Jesus arose from the dead on the third day after He died upon the cross; and if you are saved, you know that Jesus lives in you. We know that Jesus lives and that one day, the King of Kings will rule over all. Thank you, Lord, that you have imparted to me the knowledge of you, that you live, and you will one day reign!

_____

Daily Reading: 1 Corinthians 4-6

November 27

Psalm 50:2 "Out of Zion, the perfection of beauty, God hath shined."

Out of Zion… God hath shined. God shines out of Zion through His Son, Jesus Christ, the perfect man, sinless and obedient in all things for God, even suffering death on the cross. Jesus said that if you have seen Him, you have seen the Father (John 14:7). Thank you, Lord, for giving us Jesus, that in knowing Him we can also know you!

_____
_____
_____
_____
_____
_____
_____
_____

Daily Reading: 1 Corinthians 7-10

November 28

1 Thessalonians 4:16 "For the Lord himself shall descend from heaven with a shout, with the voice of the archangel, and with the trump of God: and the dead in Christ shall rise first."

For the Lord himself shall descend from heaven... and the dead in Christ shall rise first. I hear many people say they hope they are still on this earth when the Lord returns, but this tells us that the saved who have died will be called to Jesus first. Thank you, Lord, that if I die before that day of your returning, that I will be among the first to be called up to you, right out of the grave!

_____
_____
_____
_____
_____
_____
_____
_____

Daily Reading: 1 Corinthians 11-13

November 29

1 Thessalonians 4:17 "Then we which are alive and remain shall be caught up together with them in the clouds, to meet the Lord in the air: and so shall we ever be with the Lord."

We which are alive and remain shall be caught up together... to meet the Lord in the air. What a glorious meeting takes place when the Lord returns! This is the hope for all who are saved. We are waiting for the Lord to gather His saints to Him. Thank you, Lord, that you will return to take me with all your saints into the glories of Heaven, where I will live forever with you!

Daily Reading: 1 Corinthians 14-16

November 30

Galatians 5:5 "For we through the Spirit wait for the hope of righteousness by faith."

For we... wait for the hope of righteousness. Christians eagerly await the time when each one will stand before God in judgment. We will then see that our faith was not in vain, but that Jesus has cleansed us from all sin. We will stand before God righteous and justified because of the blood of Jesus. Thank you, Lord, that I will be judged perfect before God, that my sins will be covered by the precious blood of Jesus!

___

___

___

___

___

___

___

Daily Reading: 2 Corinthians 1-3

December 1

Galatians 5:22-23 "But the fruit of the Spirit is love, joy, peace, longsuffering, gentleness, goodness, faith, meekness, temperance: against such there is no law."

But the fruit of the Spirit is love. As Christians grow in the grace and knowledge of Christ they produce "fruit". Love for lost souls, love for the brethren, and especially love for Jesus will bud and grow like a luscious apple on a tree until it becomes a thing of beauty. Thank you, Lord, for the love you have planted in my heart. May it continue to grow and develop into something beautiful for thee!

_____

_____

_____

_____

_____

_____

_____

Daily Reading: 2 Corinthians 4-7

December 2

Galatians 5:22-23 "But the fruit of the Spirit is love, joy, peace, longsuffering, gentleness, goodness, faith, meekness, temperance: against such there is no law."

But the fruit of the Spirit is... joy. Joy dwells in the heart of one who knows the Lord and who lives close to Him. Even amid trials and troubles joy occupies the heart. Once the Spirit enters a child of God nothing can destroy the delight of knowing Jesus. Thank you, Lord, for giving me joy unspeakable!

Daily Reading: 2 Corinthians 8-10

December 3

Galatians 5:22-23 "But the fruit of the Spirit is love, joy, peace, longsuffering, gentleness, goodness, faith, meekness, temperance: against such there is no law."

But the fruit of the Spirit is... peace. A peace that passes all understanding is in the heart of one who knows and loves Christ. As Jesus calmed the storm when He was in the ship with the disciples, He calms the storms of life for the believer. Thank you, Lord, for giving me peace and tranquility through my trials and troubles, for I know that you are in control of all!

Daily Reading: 2 Corinthians 11-13

December 4

Galatians 5:22-23 "But the fruit of the Spirit is love, joy, peace, longsuffering, gentleness, goodness, faith, meekness, temperance: against such there is no law."

But the fruit of the Spirit is... longsuffering. As we grow in Christ, we develop a patience and quietness, or as this verse states, longsuffering. This makes us kinder and more likely to counter meanness and hate with a gentle and loving answer. Thank you, Lord, that you have given me this heart of patient endurance that I may always respond with love!

_____
_____
_____
_____
_____
_____
_____

Daily Reading: Galatians 1-3

December 5

Galatians 5:22-23 "But the fruit of the Spirit is love, joy, peace, longsuffering, gentleness, goodness, faith, meekness, temperance: against such there is no law."

But the fruit of the Spirit is…gentleness. Jesus possessed a loving gentleness when He walked this earth. He loved children, He healed those who came to Him sick and afflicted, and when He was suffering and near death on the cross, He cared for His mother, telling John to keep her and care for her. Thank you, Lord, for the spirit of gentleness. Help me to show that tenderness to others as you did!

Daily Reading: Galatians 4-6

December 6

Galatians 5:22-23 "But the fruit of the Spirit is love, joy, peace, longsuffering, gentleness, goodness, faith, meekness, temperance: against such there is no law."

But the fruit of the Spirit is… goodness. As Christians, our daily lives should reflect goodness, honor, and virtue, that others may see Jesus working in us. We should strive to always be above reproach so as not to present a stumbling block to those who are lost. Thank you, Lord, for your goodness. Let it shine forth to others through me!

Daily Reading: Ephesians 1-3

December 7

Galatians 5:22-23 "But the fruit of the Spirit is love, joy, peace, longsuffering, gentleness, goodness, faith, meekness, temperance: against such there is no law."

But the fruit of the Spirit is… faith. As we see Jesus perform wondrous works in our lives our faith grows and strengthens. We become less secure in our own abilities and depend upon God to work in us. We become less self-confident, and more God-confident. Thank you, Lord, for revealing your working in my life. Help me to depend on you for all!

_____
_____
_____
_____
_____
_____
_____

Daily Reading: Ephesians 4-6

December 8

Galatians 5:22-23 "But the fruit of the Spirit is love, joy, peace, longsuffering, gentleness, goodness, faith, meekness, temperance: against such there is no law."

But the fruit of the Spirit is… meekness. The world often associates meekness with weakness. However, Godly meekness is a virtue and strength that should be greatly desired. It is a gentle kindness and consideration of others, not uplifting self. Thank you, Lord, for developing in me a submissiveness and compliance to your will and your way!

Daily Reading: Philippians 1-4

December 9

Galatians 5:22-23 "But the fruit of the Spirit is love, joy, peace, longsuffering, gentleness, goodness, faith, meekness, temperance: against such there is no law."

But the fruit of the Spirit is... temperance. Temperance is self-control, the ability to overcome the hunger for possessions, for lust, for any desires that negatively affect our loving relationship with God. As we mature as Christians we begin to see that Jesus fulfills our wants. Thank you, Lord, for being the One who satisfies my every desire!

_____

Daily Reading: Colossians 1-4

December 10

Revelation 21:4 "And God shall wipe away all tears from their eyes; and there shall be no more death, neither sorrow, nor crying, neither shall there be any more pain: for the former things are passed away."

There shall be no more death, neither sorrow, nor crying, neither shall there be any more pain. Christian, don't you look forward to this time? Sorrow and pain are such a normal part of life that it is difficult to imagine a time where they will be no more. All will be joy and peace and delight. Thank you, Lord, that you have shown me my beautiful future, a time of satisfying pleasure in your presence!

_____
_____
_____
_____
_____
_____
_____

Daily Reading: 1 Thessalonians 1-5

December 11

Psalm 37:23-24 "The steps of a good man are ordered by the LORD: and he delighteth in his way. Though he fall, he shall not be utterly cast down: for the LORD upholdeth him with his hand."

The Lord upholdeth him with his hand. The saved child of God is held firmly in the Lord's hand, never to be cast down nor cast out. Even though the Christian sins, God has secured his salvation, and nothing can change that through all eternity. Thank you, Lord, for loving me, for dying for me, for saving me forever!

_____
_____
_____
_____
_____
_____
_____

Daily Reading: 2 Thessalonians 1-3

December 12

Romans 8:28 "And we know that all things work together for good to them that love God, to them who are the called according to his purpose."

All things work together for good to them that love God. When we reflect on times of sorrow and grief in our past, we can see how God brought us through and orchestrated our life for our good and for His glory. Sometimes the pain brought growth and learning, sometimes He had something so much better for us. Thank you, Lord, for afflictions and hardships, for they are shaping me into a vessel of honor for you!

Daily Reading: 1 Timothy 1-3

December 13

Psalm 103:2-3 "Bless the LORD, O my soul, and forget not all his benefits: who forgiveth all thine iniquities; who healeth all thy diseases."

Bless the Lord... who healeth all thy diseases. As I write this the world is battling the pandemic of COVID-19, a virus that has afflicted nearly every nation in the world, killing tens of thousands. Sin is a disease that affects every human born to man, a worldwide pandemic that brings eternal death in the fires of hell. For sin sickness there is a cure—the precious blood of Jesus, shed that all who believe will be saved. Thank you, Lord, for curing my disease of sin, for making me whole!

Daily Reading: 1 Timothy 4-6

December 14

Hebrews 10:19-20 "Having therefore, brethren, boldness to enter into the holiest by the blood of Jesus, by a new and living way, which he hath consecrated for us, through the veil, that is to say, his flesh."

Having therefore brethren, boldness to enter into the holiest by the blood of Jesus. In the Old Testament only the high priest could enter the Holy of Holies, the area of the temple where God dwelt, which was separated from the other areas by a veil, or heavy curtain. When Christ died on the cross, the veil was torn in two (Matthew 27:51). Because of His Perfect Sacrifice for sin, we have direct access to the throne of God. Thank you, Lord, that I can come before you, praising and worshiping you, submitting my petitions to you!

_____

_____

_____

_____

_____

_____

Daily Reading: 2 Timothy 1-4

December 15

Hebrews 2:18 "For in that he himself hath suffered being tempted, he is able to succour them that are tempted."

He is able to succour them that are tempted. As a man on this earth Jesus faced the same temptations to sin as other men. He understands the snares that entice us. He helps us when we are lured to go against God's will. Jesus is our strength when Satan tempts us if we call out to Him. Thank you, Lord, for aiding me when Satan sets a snare for me and when he tries to coax me to go against your Word!

_____
_____
_____
_____
_____
_____
_____

Daily Reading: Titus 1-3

December 16

Psalm 115:15 "Ye are blessed of the LORD which made heaven and earth."

Ye are blessed of the Lord. God made the earth and all that is in it, the heavens and all creation. That same God provides abundant bounty to all. He promises to the saved greater blessings when we leave this world and enter His abode in Heaven. Thank you, Lord, for the many blessings you have bestowed upon me in this life and thank you for your promises of many more to come!

_____
_____
_____
_____
_____
_____
_____
_____

Daily Reading: Philemon 1, Hebrews 1-2

December 17

Romans 4:5 "But to him that worketh not, but believeth on him that justifieth the ungodly, his faith is counted for righteousness."

But to him that... believeth on him... his faith is counted for righteousness. We all have sinned, and there is nothing we can do to remove that sin, to be counted righteous. No amount of work, of giving, of sacrifice will make us worthy to enter Heaven. Only by grace through faith may we be saved, and that faith will be counted for righteousness. Thank you, Lord, for your grace and mercy on me, for I am an unworthy sinner!

Daily Reading: Hebrews 3-6

December 18

Psalm 31:24 "Be of good courage, and he shall strengthen your heart, all ye that hope in the LORD."

He shall strengthen your heart, all ye that hope in the Lord. David was a great and courageous warrior who walked with God. In his battles, David sought the Lord's guidance and help, and God strengthened him and gave him many victories. If we remain close to God, He will do the same for us. He will fight our battles and give us boldness and fortitude in the conflict. Thank you, Lord, for giving me your strength and courage, for I am weak and fearful without you!

Daily Reading: Hebrews 7-10

December 19

2 Corinthians 5:19 "To wit, that God was in Christ, reconciling the world unto himself, not imputing their trespasses unto them; and hath committed unto us the word of reconciliation."

Not imputing their trespasses unto them. Christ took upon Himself the sin of all who would believe on Him as God and Savior. When a Christian goes before God in judgment, all his sins will be erased: the lies, the sinful thoughts, the evil words, all will be forgiven and forgotten. Thank you, Jesus, for taking my sins upon yourself on the cross, that I might appear sinless when I stand before God!

Daily Reading: Hebrews 11-13

December 20

2 Timothy 2:19 "Nevertheless the foundation of God standeth sure, having this seal, The Lord knoweth them that are his. And, Let every one that nameth the name of Christ depart from iniquity."

The foundation of God standeth sure… the Lord knoweth them that are his. Christian, you can be sure that God knows you. The Good Shepherd knows His sheep. Just as a father knows and cherishes his children and they look to him for comfort and protection, we can look to God in the same manner. Thank you, Lord, my Rock, and my Deliverer, for your strong foundation!

_____
_____
_____
_____
_____
_____
_____

Daily Reading: James 1-5

December 21

Psalm 68:5 "A father of the fatherless, and a judge of the widows, is God in his holy habitation."

A father of the fatherless, and a judge of the widows. God safeguards the downtrodden and defends and protects the orphans and the widows and those who cannot defend themselves. As Christians, we should do the same, looking after the needs of those who are weak and unprotected. Thank you, Lord, for caring for me in times when I needed you most!

___

___

___

___

___

___

___

___

Daily Reading: 1 Peter 1-5

December 22

Psalm 29:11 "The LORD will give strength unto his people; the LORD will bless his people with peace."

The Lord will bless his people with peace. As prophesied in the book of Matthew, the end times will be a time of "wars and rumors of wars" (Matthew 24:6). Battles have raged somewhere in the world throughout my whole life. What a wonderful day it will be when all the fighting is over, and God blesses us with peace. Thank you, Lord, that I can look forward to the day when battles and bloodshed are ended, and I live in peace forevermore with you!

_____

_____

_____

_____

_____

_____

_____

Daily Reading: 2 Peter 1-3

December 23

Revelation 3:20 "Behold, I stand at the door, and knock: if any man hear my voice, and open the door, I will come in to him, and will sup with him, and he with me."

If any man hear my voice, and open the door, I will come in to him. God calls the lost to Him through the Gospel, as the Holy Spirit works in the heart. Man, with his free will, must respond in repentance and faith and come to Jesus for salvation. Just as Jesus healed all the sick and afflicted who came to Him when He walked this earth, He will save all who come to him for forgiveness. He will open the door. Thank you, Lord, for opening that door to me, for forgiving my sin, and for saving my soul for eternity!

_____

_____

_____

_____

_____

_____

Daily Reading: 1 John 1-5

December 24

Psalm 91:1 "He that dwelleth in the secret place of the most High shall abide under the shadow of the Almighty."

He… shall abide under the shadow of the Almighty. In this great shadow of God, He protects us. There we can hide from our enemies and be forever safe and secure. God is all powerful, greater, and stronger than any force that may come against us. If God be for us, who can be against us? Thank you, Lord, for protecting me and defending me from the evil one!

Daily Reading: 2 John 1, 3 John 1, Jude 1

December 25

2 Peter 1:15 "Moreover I will endeavor that ye may be able after my decease to have these things always in remembrance."

Ye may be able after my decease to have these things always in remembrance. Peter preached the Word of God so that those who heard it would remember it long after he was dead and gone. Scripture verses and Bible songs learned many years ago often remain in our memories for all of our lives. God's Word may be called to mind when we need the Lord to help us in times of temptations and trials. Thank you, Lord, for the preachers and teachers who have taught me your Word, that has remained in my memory to help me in times of need!

_____
_____
_____
_____
_____
_____
_____

Daily Reading: Revelation 1-3

December 26

James 1:17a "Every good gift and every perfect gift is from above, and cometh down from the Father of lights..."

Every good gift and every perfect gift is from above. Every good thing we receive is from the Lord. He gives us jobs, physical health, and intelligence that we might be employed and earn a living. God makes the crops to grow that we may have food to eat. He blesses us with family and loved ones. Thank you, Lord, for all the good things in my life, for they have all come from you!

Daily Reading: Revelation 4-6

December 27

Philippians 1:6 "Being confident of this very thing, that he which hath begun a good work in you will perform it until the day of Jesus Christ."

He which hath begun a good work in you will perform it until the day of Jesus Christ. When we are saved by grace through faith, it is a work of the Holy Spirit, and a permanent, eternal work that will keep us saved forever. Of that we may be confident! Thank you, Lord, that you have given me eternal salvation though your shed blood!

_____

_____

_____

_____

_____

_____

_____

Daily Reading: Revelation 7-9

December 28

Psalm 129:4 "The LORD is righteous: he hath cut asunder the cords of the wicked."

He hath cut asunder the cords of the wicked. Before we are saved, we are bound by the ropes of the wicked one and held captive by sin. When we accept Jesus' gift of salvation, He cuts the cords that bind us, setting us free from Satan's hold. Thank you, Lord, that you have set me free from sin and death!

_____

_____

_____

_____

_____

_____

_____

_____

Daily Reading: Revelation 10-12

December 29

2 Samuel 22:33 "God is my strength and power: and he maketh my way perfect."

God is my strength and power. Without the Lord, we may think we have strength, but when faced with strong adversity, we are powerless. However, when we rely upon God, our might is unlimited. We can face any enemy with confidence. Thank you, Lord, for your power and strength, for in you, I can do anything!

_____
_____
_____
_____
_____
_____
_____

Daily Reading: Revelation 13-15

December 30

Psalm 149:4 "For the LORD taketh pleasure in his people: he will beautify the meek with salvation."

He will beautify the meek with salvation. When a sinner comes humbly to the Lord for salvation, God gives him a new heart, and a total change occurs. The heart is made beautiful by the grace of God. Thank you, Lord, for transforming my heart, and making it beautiful for you!

Daily Reading: Revelation 16-18

December 31

I Thessalonians 5:18 "In every thing give thanks: for this is the will of God in Christ Jesus concerning you."

In every thing give thanks. If you are saved, look at all the ways the Lord has worked in you and through you. He makes a change in you and in everything you do when you have a repentant heart. Thank you, Lord, for all the many blessings you have given me! Thank you, Lord, for everything!

Daily Reading: Revelation 19-22

CPSIA information can be obtained
at www.ICGtesting.com
Printed in the USA
LVHW041419150920
666053LV00001B/73